Ten-Minute Plays
VOLUME VIII
FOR TEENS: COMEDY
10+ Format

Ten-Minute Plays

VOLUME VIII

FOR TEENS

· · ·

COMEDY

10+ Format

YOUNG ACTORS SERIES

Kristen Dabrowski

A Smith and Kraus Book

A Smith and Kraus Book
Published by Smith and Kraus, Inc.
177 Lyme Road, Hanover, NH 03755
www.SmithandKraus.com

First Edition: April 2006
10 9 8 7 6 5 4 3 2 1
Manufactured in the United States of America

Cover and text design by Julia Hill Gignoux, Freedom Hill Design

ISBN 1-57525-443-3
10-Minute Plays for Kids Series ISSN 1553-0477

CONTENTS

TO COFFEE AND CHOCOLATE
for keeping me awake and happy

INTRODUCTION

Ten-Minute Plays aims to score on many playing fields. This book contains twelve short plays. Each play then contains two scenes and four monologues. Add it up! That means that this book contains twelve plays, twenty-four scenes, and forty-eight monologues. There's a lot to choose from, but it's not overwhelming. The plays and scenes are marked clearly. Note that the text for the monologues is set in a different typeface. If you are working on a monologue and are not performing the play or scene as a whole, take the time to hear in your mind any additional lines or character responses that you need for the monologue to make sense.

Beat indicates there is a dramatic pause in the action. You will want to consider why the beat is there. Does no one know what to do? Is someone thinking?

Feel free to combine characters (so fewer actors are needed), change a character from male to female (or vice versa), or alter the text in any way that suits you. Be as creative as you like!

For each play, I've included tips for young actors and ideas for playwrights. Here's a guide to the symbols:

⟨�massk⟩ = tips for actors

✎ = ideas for playwrights

There's a lot to work with here. Actors, the tips are meant to give you some guidance and information on how to be an even finer actor. Playwrights, I've included a few of my inspirations and invite you to borrow from them to write your own plays.

At the end of each play is a section called "Talk Back!" with discussion questions. These questions are catalysts for class discussions and projects. The plays do not make moral judgments. They are intended to spark students to use their imaginations and create their own code of ethics. Even if you're not in school, "Talk Back!" can give you some additional ideas and interesting subjects to discuss.

Lastly, there are four extras in the Appendix: Character Questionnaire for Actors, Playwright's Checklist, Scene Elements Worksheet, and Exploration Games. Each activity adds dimension and depth to the plays and is intended to appeal to various learning styles.

Enjoy!

Kristen Dabrowski

FIRST JOB

4F, 2M

WHO
    FEMALES   MALES
      Alice   Ren
      Bette   Steve
      Ellen
      Mallory

WHERE Scene 1: The kitchen of a diner; Scene 2: An office.

WHEN Present day.

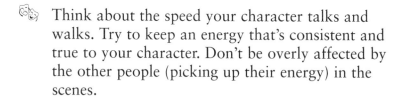 Think about the speed your character talks and walks. Try to keep an energy that's consistent and true to your character. Don't be overly affected by the other people (picking up their energy) in the scenes.

Write a scene where you give Ren another job and see how he fares.

Scene 1: Dishwasher

(STEVE and REN stand behind a table covered with dishes.)

REN: This is my first job. First day of my first job.

STEVE: Congratulations. Welcome to the wonderful world of dishwashing.

REN: I figure, how hard could it be?

(STEVE laughs.)

REN: What's so funny?

STEVE: Nothing.

REN: No, seriously. Did I say something funny?

STEVE: Nah.

REN: Come on, man. I could use some advice here, since it's my first day.

STEVE: You'll find out soon enough. Don't worry.

(ELLEN enters.)

ELLEN: *(Agitated.)* We don't have any spoons!

(ELLEN exits.)

REN: Wow. She's uptight.

(STEVE laughs.)

REN: What?

STEVE: Nothing.

REN: Don't we have spoons clean already?

STEVE: Yeah. Set them out front so they stop—

(BETTE enters.)

BETTE: I cannot serve ice cream without spoons! We need spoons! Now!

(BETTE exits.)

STEVE: —yelling at us.

REN: OK. I'll get them out there.

(REN exits with a container.)

STEVE: Poor kid doesn't know what he got himself into.

(REN enters.)

REN: OK. Done! So, anyhow, I took this job because there's this car I want. It used to be my cousin's and he said I could have it for a couple hundred, so that's why I'm working this summer. I could really use a car. Do you have a car?

STEVE: My dad gave me his old one.

REN: That's cool.

STEVE: Well, it's a car.

REN: Exactly. I figure if I can just get out on the road, I'll be that much closer to freedom, you know?

STEVE: I guess.

REN: You're kind of negative. You having a bad day or something?

STEVE: No. A day like all others.

(MALLORY enters.)

MALLORY: Where is José?

STEVE: There is no José.

MALLORY: You know, the chef guy?

STEVE: You mean Juan.

MALLORY: Whatever! That guy. Where is he?

STEVE: How should I know?

MALLORY: Well, have you seen him?

STEVE: No.

MALLORY: What about you, kid?

REN: No. I don't know anybody. It's my first day here. I'm Ren.

MALLORY: Hi. Well, you guys have been a lot of help. If you see José or whatever his name is, chef guy, could you tell him I need my orders? Hello? I mean this is a restaurant. We serve food. It would be nice to have a chef. It's kind of important. Aren't you guys supposed to be washing things? We didn't have any spoons for, like, twenty minutes! People were going crazy. We get ice cream and coffee orders every minute, and we had no spoons. Think about that for a minute, geniuses. I had to wipe old spoons off on my apron and hope I wasn't giving people diseases! No one seems to understand that we're on the firing line. You get to chill out back here, and we get people acting like lunatics and yelling at us nonstop every two seconds about their food being cold, their fork being dirty, and all that stuff. We have to deal with your incompetence. Please, please could you at least pretend to care about what I'm saying? Hello? Am I talking to myself here?

REN: We're working. We'll get right on it.

MALLORY: Well, new guy—

REN: Ren.

MALLORY: —Ren, maybe you're not so hopeless after all.

(MALLORY exits.)

STEVE: She's a wacko.

REN: Why is everyone so stressed? It's just food, right?

STEVE: I guess.

REN: So why is everyone so tense?

STEVE: They're wacko.

REN: Well, I guess she's right, though. We should get to work.

STEVE: Go ahead.

REN: What do you mean? Aren't you going to help?

STEVE: No.

REN: What do you mean, no?

STEVE: I mean nah. I don't think so.

REN: So you expect me to do all the work?

STEVE: Do it, don't do it . . . Whatever. Like I care.

REN: How do things get clean around here then?

STEVE: Every hour or so I'll just run the hose over the dishes and stuff. That's all.

REN: But that doesn't get them clean, does it?

STEVE: I use hot water.

REN: And that works?

STEVE: If it does, it does. If it doesn't . . .

REN: If it doesn't—what?

STEVE: Whatever. Doesn't matter to me.

REN: Isn't that unhygienic? I mean, I wouldn't want to eat off those dishes.

STEVE: That's why I don't eat here. I eat fries off of napkins, but that's it.

REN: This might sound weird, but don't you take any pride in your job?

STEVE: You're kidding, right? I wash dishes, dude. I don't save the world or anything. This is a sucky job. I do it because my dad says I have to learn the value of a dollar. And that's pretty much exactly what it pays. I get about a dollar at the end of the week after putting in loads of hours when any normal teenager is out at the beach or whatever with his friends. If you think you are going to get a car with your paycheck, you are really out of touch with reality. You are going to sit in this kitchen all day, day after day after day after day, with the waitresses yelling at you, sweating to death, and you're going to get paid a pathetic excuse for a salary for your trouble. So, as I see it, there are two choices. Do as little as possible and make your life easier, or work your ass off and still get the same lousy paycheck. It's up to you. But I've made my choice.

REN: Are you serious?

STEVE: Do I look like I'm kidding?

REN: But doesn't it add up?

STEVE: The money? They take out taxes, dude. You're left with nothing.

REN: Are you serious?

STEVE: I couldn't be more serious.

REN: Then why are you here?

STEVE: I told you, my dad makes me. I would not be here otherwise. And I get his old car as long as I work. It's as big as a boat and it always breaks down, but it's a car. But if I quit, he takes it away.

REN: Oh.

STEVE: It's not all bad, though. Some of the other kitchen guys are cool. Sometimes when we want to piss off the waitresses, we'll put a hair in something, just to see if someone will notice and yell at them. And we spit in things.

REN: I am never eating here again.

STEVE: It's funny. And people do it at every restaurant.

REN: No, they don't!

STEVE: They totally do.

REN: I am never eating out again.

STEVE: It's funny. Have a sense of humor! It keeps the stress from getting too bad.

REN: But you don't work!

STEVE: Well, it's stressful to have people yelling at you to get to work all the time.

REN: Then why don't you do some work, then?

STEVE: Kid, you've got so much to learn. I almost feel sorry for you.

Scene 2: Office Temp

(REN is at a desk covered with papers and a telephone.)

REN: I finished putting those reports together.

ALICE: Did you do it right?

REN: I did it how you told me to do it.

ALICE: You three-hole punched the reports?

REN: Yes.

ALICE: And you put them in the folders?

REN: Yes.

ALICE: The *red* folders?

REN: I did what you told me to do.

ALICE: Did you put the stickers on the front?

REN: I did exactly what you told me to do.

ALICE: **Are you giving me attitude? Because I don't need attitude.**

REN: I'm just answering you. There's no reason why you would know this, we just met today, but I'm actually pretty smart.

ALICE: Well, that's wonderful for you.

REN: I'm just saying I can collate papers pretty easily.

ALICE: Well, I certainly hope so. If these reports aren't organized right, my head is going to be on the line. These are very important clients and Mr. Beatty wants everything to be perfect. I am his right-hand woman so I am responsible for this going off without a hitch.

REN: I understand.

ALICE: I don't know that you do. If there's any mistake—

REN: It will be bad. For you. For the clients. For Mr. Beatty. I understand.

ALICE: Give me the reports. I'll check them in the office.

(REN hands ALICE a stack of red folders.)

ALICE: I just hope they're right. I don't have time to do them again. I've got a million things to do. I'm terribly busy.

REN: They're right. I'm sure. I double-checked.

(ALICE begins to exit.)

REN: What should I do now, Alice?

ALICE: I don't have time to show you anything else right now. Just answer the phone lines. You remember how I told you to answer the phone? You have to say "Good afternoon, Mr. Beatty's office." Can you remember that?

REN: I can remember that.

ALICE: I can't chat like this anymore. I've got to go do some work. No more socializing for you either! Get to work. I'll check back to see your progress later.

(ALICE exits.)

REN: Progress? I'm answering the phone. I think I know how to do that. I have been alive on the face of the earth for a while now. God, it's not like I'm stupid or anything.

(The phone rings. REN picks it up.)

REN: Hello, Mr. Beatty's office . . . OK, just a moment . . .

(REN hangs up the phone.)

REN: Alice? Alice!

(ALICE enters.)

ALICE: What is it? I'm busy.

REN: There's a Mr. Schwartz on the phone for Mr. Beatty. How do I transfer the call?

ALICE: You don't. Mr. Beatty doesn't want to speak to Mr. Schwartz today.

REN: OK.

(ALICE *begins to exit.*)

REN: Oh—wait!

ALICE: What is it?

REN: What should I tell him?

ALICE: Tell him Mr. Beatty is in a meeting and can't speak to him.

REN: OK.

ALICE: Take his name and number down on the message pad and tell him Mr. Beatty will call him back tomorrow. Which, of course, he won't.

REN: OK.

(ALICE *exits.* REN *hits a button on the phone.*)

REN: Mr. Beatty? I mean, Mr. Schwartz? Hello? Hello?

(REN *punches some buttons on the phone.*)

REN: Where did he go?

(ALICE *enters.*)

ALICE: Is everything OK?

REN: Yeah. I guess Mr. Schwartz hung up.

ALICE: Did you put him on hold?

REN: What? Oh yeah, yeah.

ALICE: Yeah, you did? Or yeah, you didn't?

REN: I did. He must have hung up.

ALICE: Well, I suppose he'll call back. Or maybe he won't and that's fine, too. After all, Mr. Beatty can't speak with him anyway. At any rate, I noticed a mistake in these reports.

REN: You're kidding.

ALICE: No, I'm not kidding. I don't kid.

REN: Oh. Well, what is it?

ALICE: You didn't put Mr. Beatty's business card in the front of the folder.

REN: You didn't tell me to.

ALICE: I think I did.

REN: No, really, you didn't.

ALICE: I'm sure I did.

REN: But I don't even have any of his business cards. How could I put his business cards in the folder if I don't have any?

ALICE: Open the middle drawer in your desk.

(REN opens the middle drawer in the desk.)

ALICE: What do you see?

REN: Boxes.

ALICE: What's in those boxes?

REN: They're closed.

ALICE: Open them, please, Ren.

(REN opens a box.)

REN: Business cards.

ALICE: See why you need to listen?

REN: But—

ALICE: I'll bring the folders back. You may want to check your list again to make sure you did the other steps correctly as well.

(ALICE exits. REN pulls out his list.)

REN: "Collate pages. Put in numerical order. Make sure pages all face the same direction." What does she think I am? A moron?

(The phone rings.)

REN: Hello? Mr. Schwartz's office . . . Oh, Mr. Schwartz! . . . Of course I meant Mr. Beatty's office . . . Sorry we got disconnected before . . . Mr. Beatty's in a meeting and he can't come to the phone . . . It's important? . . . But he's in a meeting . . .

I don't think I can interrupt . . . But . . . OK, just a minute, I'll check.

(REN nearly hangs up again, then at the last minute remembers to put the call on hold. ALICE enters.)

ALICE: Here are the reports. Put the business card—

REN: Alice?

ALICE: What is it?

REN: Mr. Schwartz is on the phone again.

ALICE: I told you to tell him that Mr. Beatty is in a meeting and can't come to the phone.

REN: I told him that.

ALICE: So?

REN: So he says he still wants to speak to him. He wants me to interrupt Mr. Beatty's meeting.

ALICE: You can't do that. It's important.

REN: I told him that. He said what he had to tell Mr. Beatty was very important, too. Urgent.

ALICE: Well, Mr. Beatty just can't speak to him. I can't hold your hand about everything, Ren. You have to start taking on some responsibilities. This is a job, not a walk in the park.

REN: I know.

ALICE: So, as I was saying, put the business cards in the folders and go over your directions, please. We can't afford to have these mistakes again. I need these folders back in ten minutes, OK?

REN: OK. No problem.

(ALICE exits. REN gets out the business cards. The phone rings.)

REN: Hello? Mr. Beatty's office? . . .

(ALICE reenters.)

REN: What can I help you with, sir? I'm afraid Mr. Beatty is in a meeting. He can't be disturbed. May I take a message? . . . Thank you, sir. I will be sure he gets the message. *(Hangs up the phone.)* Oh! Mr. Schwartz! *(Presses a button on the phone.)* Mr. Schwartz? I'm sorry. Mr. Beatty just can't speak to you . . . No. I'm sorry, sir. He can't be disturbed just now. I tried, sir. May I take a message? . . . No? You'll call back? . . . But if I take a message then he can call you when he's free . . . No? OK. Bye. *(Hangs up.)* He didn't want me to take a message.

ALICE: It would be better if you took a message.

REN: I tried. He didn't want me to take a message.

ALICE: Who was the other call from?

REN: Mr. John Truss.

ALICE: John Truss? Vice president of Shotz and Macklefecker?

REN: I guess so.

ALICE: You guess so?

REN: He didn't say the company.

ALICE: And you didn't ask?

REN: No.

ALICE: He's only the most important client. Mr. Beatty wants to speak to him immediately whenever he calls!

REN: I didn't know.

ALICE: Well, he's only the vice president—But you wouldn't know that because you didn't ask.

REN: Sorry. I didn't know.

ALICE: Give me the message. I'm going to have to try to smooth this over with Mr. Beatty.

(REN hands ALICE the message.)

ALICE: Are you done with those folders?

REN: You just gave them to me.

ALICE: You'd better hurry up then.

(ALICE exits. REN picks up the phone and dials.)

REN: Hi, Mom? It's Ren. Listen, this job isn't work-
    ing out either. I know I said that last time, but
    they were spitting on the dishes in that restau-
    rant. I couldn't be a part of that! *(Beat.)* Well,
    here . . . I just don't think I'm very good at this,
    Mom. I don't seem to be able to do anything
    right. And everyone treats me like I'm stupid.
    There's this girl here, she thinks she's my boss,
    but she's, like, a year older than me . . . She's
    just really mean and bossy, Mom. I don't like
    this. *(Beat.)* I don't know; maybe I'm just not
    meant to work. Maybe it's just not me. I don't
    need a car that bad. *(Beat.)* When I graduate? I
    don't know. I could just help you out around the
    house. You're always saying you need more help.
    And I could play guitar, maybe get in a band or
    something. But work, Mom? It's just not me.
    There's got to be another way. I'm not a quitter,
    but I'm sorry. I quit. Can you pick me up and
    drive me home now? *(Beat.)* I know it's only
    eleven-fifteen. But can you please come soon,
    Mom?

TALK BACK!

1. Which was the better job?

2. How do you know when to quit something and when to keep going?

3. Should work be hard and stressful?

4. Do you look forward to entering the working world? Why or why not?

5. As a boss, is it better to manage a new employee closely or trust them to do the job right?

6. If you work hard, you'll just get more work. True or false?

7. If you do less, people will expect less. What do you think of this philosophy?

FIGHTING FOR LOVE

2F, 2M

WHO

FEMALES
> Miranda
> Sylvie

MALES
> Faber
> Spence

WHERE A school lunchroom.

WHEN Scene 1: Between classes; Scene 2: Between classes, one week later.

🎭 Comedy requires fearlessness. Don't be afraid to go too far. Commit fully to everything you do and say. If you're worried about looking stupid, people will laugh *at* you and not *with* you. Go for it!

✎ One classic setup in romantic comedy is to get two different personality types together. Make up two very different characters and see if you can make them fall in love. Make sure the road to romance is bumpy.

Scene 1: Untrue

MIRANDA: You should apologize to me.

FABER: Why?

MIRANDA: You were rude.

FABER: When?

MIRANDA: You said my idea was stupid.

FABER: Your idea was stupid.

MIRANDA: You're not supposed to say that to a person.

FABER: Even if it's true?

MIRANDA: It wasn't true.

FABER: It was!

MIRANDA: It wasn't! And anyway, you're just not supposed to talk to people like that. It was disrespectful.

FABER: Like you never say things like that to me.

MIRANDA: I don't!

FABER: You said in class today something like, "That's blatantly false and you'd know that if you had a brain in your head."

MIRANDA: I did not say that!

FABER: You did. Maybe not just like that—

MIRANDA: So therefore I didn't say that!

FABER: —*but* you did definitely say that part about me being brainless.

MIRANDA: I didn't say you were brainless, I just said if you had a brain you'd know—

FABER: Which implies that I'm brainless!

MIRANDA: What's your point?

FABER: What's *your* point?

MIRANDA: That you're rude and disrespectful.

FABER: And that's my point, too! You're the same way.

MIRANDA: But I'm a girl.

FABER: So that makes it OK?

MIRANDA: So it makes you worse.

FABER: That's crap!

MIRANDA: You are so infantile!

FABER: Takes one to know one!

MIRANDA: Thank you for making my point!

FABER: You're welcome!

SPENCE: Uh, Faber? We have chemistry now.

FABER: Good! Because I'd rather handle acid than talk to her any longer!

MIRANDA: Ditto!

FABER: Very creative!

MIRANDA: I know!

(FABER and SPENCE exit.)

SYLVIE: Wow.

MIRANDA: I know. Can you believe him?

SYLVIE: No, I was thinking about you.

MIRANDA: What about me?

SYLVIE: You're being a little obvious.

MIRANDA: About what? How much I hate him?

SYLVIE: No! How much you love him.

MIRANDA: What?!

SYLVIE: You heard me.

MIRANDA: I love him like I like warts or chicken pox or acne.

SYLVIE: Please.

MIRANDA: I'm serious! How in the world could you ever think I even remotely like him?

SYLVIE: You want his attention so badly, it's insane.

MIRANDA: I want some respect, that's all.

SYLVIE: Did you notice that you stand really close to him when you fight?

MIRANDA: If I don't get in his face, he doesn't listen to me.

SYLVIE: *(Doubtfully.)* Mmm-hmm.

MIRANDA: You really think—Then you have to explain this to me better because I do not have anything but disgust for Faber.

SYLVIE: You're really sticking to this "I hate him" story?

MIRANDA: It's no story.

SYLVIE: OK. If that's what you want to do.

MIRANDA: Get on with it, Sylvie. Spill it. Explain this theory of yours.

SYLVIE: For starters, you're always talking to him, even though you claim to hate him. You say things to hj purposely push his buttons.

MIRANDA: Like what?

SYLVIE: Like you're always telling him what a baby he is and calling him a girl and such.

MIRANDA: He is.

SYLVIE: I think you want him to go caveman on you. You want him to grab you and press his man-flesh against you!

MIRANDA: No way! Absolutely no way! That is vile!

SYLVIE: You get all tense when he's around. When you talk to him you get red in the face, you know that?

MIRANDA: I'm *mad*, Sylvie.

SYLVIE: You're blushing.

MIRANDA: What—

SYLVIE: Let me finish! And you get really excited when you argue with him. It's like you enjoy it. Like it fires you up.

MIRANDA: All right. I have had enough of this. That is truly disgusting. I am not talking to you anymore.

SYLVIE: I'm just calling it like I see it. You love him.

MIRANDA: I hate him!

SYLVIE: Right.

MIRANDA: You say that like you still don't believe it.

SYLVIE: I don't know. Maybe you don't even know you love him yet. But you do. Think about it, Miranda. You're in a lot of the same classes. You both love to debate. God, do you love to debate. It gets so boring listening to you two go on and on sometimes. Except that it eats up a lot of class time. But you get all hot and bothered about the same things—books, politics, religion, ethics. Did it ever occur to you that you'd be good together if you could ever shut your mouth? Maybe he might even kiss you. I think if you didn't give him such a hard time, he might like you. It's not like he's the regular girl's type of guy. He's fairly cute, but talks a lot, he thinks he knows everything—And you're a know-it-all bigmouth, too. So it's perfect. Do you really not see this? Because it is just so obvious, Miranda. It's obvious to everyone but you. To tell you the truth, I don't know which I'd like to see more: you two get together or you two just kill each other and be done with it. Whatever would get you to shut up. I swear, it's stressful to be around you.

MIRANDA: What planet are you from? What did you do with Sylvie? You are like some kind of crazy pod creature. I feel like you're speaking an entirely different language. That we're from different planets!

SYLVIE: I get it. You think I'm nuts.

MIRANDA: You're completely nuts! OK. I'm going to try to be logical about this. How can I say this? Faber. Is. Yucky. I'm serious. I like him as much as I like the toad I had to dissect in biology class. Sylvie, I'm serious. If I turn red when I talk to him, it's because I'm mad. If I stand closer to him, it's because I think he's deaf sometimes. And maybe we are interested in the same things, but we are on total opposite sides of every issue! I would like to think that I have enough sense to know that opposites do *not* attract. I want a guy who is not so stuffy and conservative and reactionary and—God!—yucky! What can I say to make you believe that I am not interested in Faber? Because I am *not* interested in Faber. *(Beat.)* Do you really think he's cute?

SYLVIE: Pretty cute.

MIRANDA: Faber?

SYLVIE: Yeah. Were we talking about anyone else for the past five minutes?

MIRANDA: Seriously, Faber?

SYLVIE: He's not my type, but I can see how someone could like him. Someone like you.

MIRANDA: What does that mean? He's not good enough for you, but he's good enough for me?

SYLVIE: No. Take it easy! I meant that I like bad boys, the dangerous type. But you like the brains more. I want to ride a motorcycle; you want to watch a foreign film. Know what I mean? We just want different things. And I think Faber would watch a foreign film, take you to dinner—all that stuff.

MIRANDA: Whatever.

SYLVIE: Think about it, Miranda. I think he's exactly what you want in a guy only you don't know it. How can smart people be so dumb? I swear, it's always true. The smarter you are about books, the dumber you are about people.

MIRANDA: Thanks a lot.

SYLVIE: I'll give you this one for free. Trust me. I know what I'm talking about.

MIRANDA: What a friend.

Scene 2: Unfalse

MIRANDA: So you have to help me with this.

SYLVIE: I'm glad you finally came to your senses.

MIRANDA: That's funny because I feel like I've gone completely crazy.

SYLVIE: That's love, Miranda. Butterflies in the stomach are a must.

MIRANDA: Well, I think it's more like pterodactyls in my stomach.

SYLVIE: You are one weird kid.

MIRANDA: OK, OK! So what should I do?

SYLVIE: Well, he's supposed to come out of this classroom any minute now.

MIRANDA: Right.

SYLVIE: When he does, you talk to him.

MIRANDA: What do I say?

SYLVIE: Hi.

MIRANDA: Right. Then what?

SYLVIE: Then you let him talk.

MIRANDA: Right, right, right. But how do we get from "hi" to him asking me out?

SYLVIE: Well, you need to take this one step at a time. You need to just show him you're interested now.

MIRANDA: But I don't like waiting. The prom is coming up. We need to get this going now.

SYLVIE: Then you might need to ask him out.

MIRANDA: I couldn't do that.

SYLVIE: Why not?

MIRANDA: What if he said no?

SYLVIE: He might, since you've been so mean to him before. That's why I told you to lay the groundwork.

MIRANDA: There's no time for groundwork! Groundwork is for losers!

SYLVIE: Well then, I don't know what to tell you. You don't want groundwork and you don't want to ask him out.

MIRANDA: **I thought you said you thought he was interested in me?**

SYLVIE: Well, he might be. He should be. Just like you should be interested in him. You're like the same person. It's creepy.

MIRANDA: **But you're not sure? I thought you were sure! You said you were sure!**

SYLVIE: Calm down. Jesus, Miranda, you've gone over the edge. You have to act calm.

MIRANDA: But I'm never calm. That's just not me. I've never been calm in my whole life. How am I supposed to start now? Do guys like calm girls? Because if they do, I'm doomed. I may as well live underground like a mole person.

SYLVIE: A mole person?

MIRANDA: I don't know! I can't stop talking! What's wrong with me? I think I'm having a heart attack. I've got pterodactyls in my stomach and my heart is stopping. It's all clogged with junk, just like my head! I don't want to feel this way. This is your fault! Yours! You made me see that I like him. Before, I was happy just hating him. Just fighting. And now, now—I'm crazy! I'm out of my mind with—oh, God, it's hideous!—love! This is wrong. I'm bailing out. See what's become of me? I'm a wreck! I'm—I'm—I'm—stuttering! I'm going to have to go through speech therapy! Maybe this is a stroke. Maybe I had a stroke! Maybe I'm only going to be able to talk out of one side of my face now and no one will ever love me! I hate you, Sylvie! This is all your fault!

(SYLVIE covers MIRANDA's mouth.)

SYLVIE: Listen to me. He will come out of this room. You will say hi. He will say hi. You will ask him how it's going. He will answer you. You will say that you are having problems with your English homework—

MIRANDA: I never have problems with my English homework!

SYLVIE: *(Covers MIRANDA's mouth)* —You will *pretend* you are having problems with your English homework—

MIRANDA: But I'm smart!

SYLVIE: *(Takes her hand off MIRANDA's mouth and wipes it on her pants.)* Jeez, you drooled on me, Miranda!

MIRANDA: I am not going to pretend I'm dumb.

SYLVIE: Well then, if you're so smart, *you* think of a way to get him to go out with you in a way that doesn't seem like a date.

MIRANDA: You have a point.

(The door opens. SPENCE and FABER enter.)

SYLVIE: Spence!

SPENCE: *(Surprised.)* Hi!

SYLVIE: I need to talk to you.

SPENCE: I gotta talk to Faber about our experiment.

SYLVIE: Spence. I need to talk to you.

SPENCE: You never talk to me.

SYLVIE: Spence! I need to talk to you!

SPENCE: So talk! What do you want!

SYLVIE: I need to talk to you alone.

SPENCE: Why?

SYLVIE: Because I do.

SPENCE: That's not an answer.

SYLVIE: Well, you need to go over there to hear the answer.

SPENCE: But I don't think I care about the answer.

SYLVIE: Spence, I swear I'm going to hit you. Come over here now!

SPENCE: No way!

SYLVIE: Why are you being so difficult?

SPENCE: You scare me.

SYLVIE: You haven't even seen scary yet. Let's go.

SPENCE: But I have to talk to Faber.

SYLVIE: I don't think so.

(SYLVIE drags SPENCE offstage.)

FABER: What was that?

MIRANDA: I don't know.

(SPENCE reenters, looking disheveled.)

SPENCE: Help, Faber!

(*SYLVIE reaches in and grabs SPENCE, dragging him offstage yet again. After a beat, SPENCE comes back onstage again.*)

SPENCE: I don't know what happened to her. She's gone nuts. She's clawing at me like a wild she-beast!

(*SYLVIE walks calmly and slowly back onstage. She looks at SPENCE for a beat. SPENCE looks back at her. Suddenly, SPENCE runs off in the opposite direction with SYLVIE right on his heels.*)

FABER: Does she like him?

MIRANDA: I don't think so. We . . . we were just talking about English homework, you know? And we were saying how we didn't really get it.

FABER: You didn't get it?

MIRANDA: No. Well, I'm not *exactly* sure.

FABER: Oh my God. Miranda doesn't know something!

MIRANDA: Shut up.

FABER: Fine. I gotta go anyway.

MIRANDA: So, I think Sylvie wanted to ask Spence about the homework.

FABER: Spence is good at science, not English.

MIRANDA: So maybe you could help instead.

FABER: Help Sylvie?

MIRANDA: No, me.

FABER: Me?

MIRANDA: Yes.

FABER: No.

MIRANDA: What?

FABER: No.

MIRANDA: Why?

FABER: Because! Do you really need me to explain, Miranda?

MIRANDA: I guess so.

FABER: You are acting so strange today.

MIRANDA: Am I?

FABER: Yes!

MIRANDA: Well? So? Explain.

FABER: We don't get along. At all.

MIRANDA: Sure we do.

FABER: Oh my God. Who are you?

MIRANDA: Miranda.

FABER: I don't think so.

MIRANDA: Believe it. I don't have a twin.

FABER: Are you sure? Because that would explain a lot.

MIRANDA: I think it's a good idea.

FABER: A twin?

MIRANDA: Working together on English homework. I mean, we do well separately, so we'd do even better together, right? Two great brains rolled into one.

FABER: Three.

MIRANDA: Three?

FABER: Sylvie, remember?

MIRANDA: Well, it would probably be easier if we worked on it together, since we work at the same pace, and then I explained it to Sylvie.

FABER: Ah, but we're back at square one. We don't get along, Miranda.

MIRANDA: Sure we do. We just debate.

FABER: Debate? I would call it fighting. Or arguing at the very least!

MIRANDA: What are you talking about We just both like to debate, that's all. I like foreign films, do you?

FABER: What? Well, yes and no. Not all of them.

MIRANDA: No, of course.

FABER: There's this film out of Korea now you'd hate, but I'm totally dying to see.

MIRANDA: I bet I'd like it.

FABER: I bet you wouldn't.

MIRANDA: I bet I would.

FABER: Do you like graphic violence?

MIRANDA: Well . . . some.

FABER: No, you don't.

MIRANDA: No, I don't.

FABER: And you can do your own English homework.

MIRANDA: I know.

FABER: So what's up with you?

(SPENCE enters, looking as though he's been attacked by a she-beast.)

SPENCE: You guys, I'm in love.

FABER/MIRANDA: What?

SPENCE: I'm in love with Sylvie.

FABER/MIRANDA: What!?

SPENCE: She's perfect. Fiery. So angry! The way she dug her fingers into my shoulder . . . I hope this bruise never heals. I didn't think a girl like her could like a guy like me. I have to be honest here. I've always hoped to have what you two have. Whenever I'd see you debating in classes and between classes and after school and at school functions, I'd think, "Wow, I wish I could have a love like that." And now, I think I've met my match at last. But it wasn't at all what I thought it would be. I thought I wanted a meeting of the minds, but no! I want . . . her. Something primal. Something instinctual. Something . . . animal. My life is complete. I live only for the next moment when I see her eyebrows meet in rage. I am in love!

(SPENCE exits, dazed.)

FABER: What was that? Why do people think we like each other? We don't. *(Beat.)* Miranda? *(Beat.)* We hate each other, right?

MIRANDA: Everyone says you like me.

FABER: That's crazy. It's obvious that if anyone likes anyone here, it's you liking me.

MIRANDA: Please. That is pathetic.

FABER: Takes one to know one.

MIRANDA: Very mature. You're an idiot.

FABER: I know you are, but what am I?

MIRANDA: You are so hot.

FABER: I know you are, but what am I? Wait—

MIRANDA: I *knew* you liked me.

FABER: What? You tricked me.

MIRANDA: You wish.

   (Lights fade as MIRANDA and FABER argue.)

TALK BACK!

1. Do opposites attract? Or are people attracted to people with similar interests?

2. Is arguing an indication of interest or antagonism?

3. Should Faber and Miranda be together? How about Spence and Sylvie?

4. Why is the phrase "drives me crazy" given both negative (aggressive) and positive (romantic) meanings?

5. Does love come from the head or somewhere else? Can you decide you're in love or do you just know it by the way you feel?

6. Do you know any couples that constantly debate? Why do you think they do this?

7. What do you do to get someone's attention if you're interested?

8. Is Sylvie right—are smart people dumb about relationships?

ACROSS THE POND SCUM

3F, 4M

WHO

FEMALES	MALES
Carina	Dell
Mary	Linus
Shannen	Principal Nyland
	Tex

WHERE A school hallway.

WHEN Present day.

📖 When you're working on an accent, begin by introducing just a few sound changes and add on more as you improve. It's more important (and convincing) to be consistent with just a few pronunciation rules than to fade in and out of the accent.

✎ Write a scene in a dialect. See if you can pick up the rhythm, sounds, and flavor of the accent. For an added challenge, set the scene in another country. Do your research and transport the performers and audience to another place!

Scene 1: Import

LINUS: So, you're new. Where are you from?

TEX: England.

LINUS: How come your name is Tex?

TEX: My father liked old cowboy movies.

LINUS: Is he dead?

TEX: No, he's alive. He still likes those movies, I guess.

LINUS: That's kind of strange. That would be like my dad calling me Lord Castleton or something.

TEX: I suppose.

LINUS: So, what's England like?

TEX: Rainy.

LINUS: It's rainy here, too!

TEX: Great.

LINUS: So where are you from in England?

TEX: Um, London.

LINUS: The capital! That's the capital, right?

TEX: Right.

LINUS: How come you moved here?

TEX: My father's job.

LINUS: Right. That makes sense.

(MARY and SHANNEN enter, acting a little giggly.)

SHANNEN: Hi there.

LINUS: Hi, girls!

MARY: Hi.

SHANNEN: Introduce us to your friend, Linus.

LINUS: Oh! OK. Girls, this is Tex.

TEX: Hello.

MARY: Linus, tell him our names, too!

LINUS: Oh! OK. Tex, this is Mary and Shannen.

TEX: Pleased to meet you.

SHANNEN: Your accent is nice.

TEX: Thank you.

MARY: So how come you're named Tex?

LINUS: His dad likes cowboy movies.

SHANNEN: Oh. Do you like it here?

LINUS: Well, it rains a lot in England, too, so he'll probably be right at home.

MARY: So where are you from in England?

LINUS: He's from London. It's the capital.

MARY: I know that!

LINUS: Oh.

SHANNEN: Linus, will you let him talk for himself?

MARY: We want to hear his voice.

SHANNEN: We've heard yours, like, a million times already.

LINUS: Right!

SHANNEN: What brings you here?

LINUS: His dad's—Sorry.

TEX: My father's job.

MARY: What does he do?

TEX: Financial things—banking and such.

MARY: "And such"!

SHANNEN: That is so cute.

LINUS: Why do you girls go so crazy over guys with accents?

MARY: I don't know.

SHANNEN: It's chemical or something.

LINUS: If I went over to England, would the girls go all crazy for my accent?

TEX: Your accent? Probably not.

LINUS: Oh. How come?

TEX: I'm not sure. I think they'd probably rather hear an Italian accent.

MARY: Ooo, Italian!

LINUS: I just don't get it. Well, I've got to run. In this country, Tex, that doesn't mean I'll actually run. It just means I have to leave.

TEX: I see.

SHANNEN: He's not dumb, Linus.

LINUS: He's foreign! I'm just trying to help.

TEX: Thank you, Linus.

LINUS: No problem. See you tomorrow!

   (LINUS exits.)

TEX: So now I have you ladies to myself.

MARY: *(Giggling.)* I guess so!

SHANNEN: Oh my God, you are so cute!

TEX: Thank you. I've always had a thing for pretty American girls. I consider myself quite fortunate to have ended up at this school.

MARY: You like American girls?

TEX: Very much.

SHANNEN: Oh my God, you are so, so cute!

(PRINCIPAL NYLAND enters.)

PRINCIPAL NYLAND: Tex, may I speak with you a moment? Ladies, will you excuse our new student?

MARY: *(Sighing.)* OK.

SHANNEN: If we have to.

(MARY and SHANNON exit, looking longingly at TEX. TEX crosses to where PRINCIPAL NYLAND is standing.)

PRINCIPAL NYLAND: How is your first day going, Tex? How do you like it here?

TEX: *(Speaking in an Texas accent.)* Fine, sir.

PRINCIPAL NYLAND: And everything's going OK?

TEX: Yes, sir.

PRINCIPAL NYLAND: It must be a bit of a shock, coming up here from the south.

TEX: No, sir. Everything's fine. But, if I may say so, I'd just as soon keep my past behind me.

PRINCIPAL NYLAND: Why's that, son? Did you get in trouble back at home? I don't recall seeing it in your records . . .

TEX: No, sir, it's just that this place is my home now. The past is the past.

PRINCIPAL NYLAND: You've got a good attitude, Tex. That will take you far.

TEX: Thank you, sir.

PRINCIPAL NYLAND: Tex, you don't need to call me sir. Call me Principal Nyland.

TEX: You've got it, sir.

PRINCIPAL NYLAND: You've got a great future ahead of you, Tex.

TEX: Thank you, Principal Nyland, sir.

(PRINCIPAL NYLAND exits.)

TEX: That was a close call.

(CARINA enters.)

CARINA: Tex?

TEX: Yep? I mean . . . *(With an English accent.)* Yes?

CARINA: I hear you're from England.

TEX: That's correct.

CARINA: So am I!

TEX: Really? What a . . . small world.

CARINA: Precisely! Where are you from, Tex?

TEX: I'm from London.

CARINA: Brilliant! So am I! What part of London?

TEX: The . . . center part.

CARINA: What stop on the tube?

TEX: Sorry? I was thinking about my . . . I left my math book somewhere . . .

CARINA: What stop on the underground line are you on?

TEX: Where did I leave that book . . .

CARINA: The subway stop nearest you in London?

TEX: Oh, the tube! Well, I . . . I don't take the tube.

CARINA: Aren't you posh? Your parents must have gobs of cash! I took the tube everywhere! Do you take taxis then?

TEX: Yes.

CARINA: Have you been to America a lot?

TEX: What? No. I mean, some, of course, with my father's work.

CARINA: I could tell. Your accent is . . . unusual.

TEX: Is it?

CARINA: Sort of muddled.

TEX: Is that so?

CARINA: Yeah.

TEX: Like you said, must be my time in America.

CARINA: I'm from Clapham.

TEX: Uh-huh.

CARINA: Have you been on the London Eye?

TEX: No. Em, my vision is quite good.

CARINA: It's a ferris wheel.

TEX: Ha, ha, ha. Kidding. That old British humor. Well, must dash.

(TEX *runs offstage.* MARY *and* SHANNEN *enter.*)

MARY: Tex?

SHANNEN: Why is he running like that?

CARINA: Because he's not English.

MARY: What do you mean?

SHANNEN: Of course he is.

CARINA: No, he's not. I doubt he's ever been to London in his whole life. He doesn't know a thing about it. I don't care how posh you are, there isn't a person alive in London who doesn't know what tube stop they're near. It's like knowing the street you live on. And he thought the London Eye was an ophthalmologist's office or something! I'm telling you, he's not for real! I'm certain of it.

MARY: Why would he lie?

CARINA: Good question. Why would he lie? Maybe he got into huge legal trouble and now he's trying to cover it up. He probably killed his parents and now he's on the run from the law. I can't believe you actually thought for a moment that a boy named Tex was English! What suckers you are! You girls are too trusting. Take it from a city girl—never trust anyone! The world is full of liars. Particularly ones named Tex! The very name sounds suspicious. He may as well be called Blagger.

SHANNEN: Blagger?

CARINA: It's what we English call a liar.

MARY: I still don't know why he'd lie. I'm sure he's not a killer. He's so cute! And I know killers don't always look like hideous freaks, but still! He's way too cute to be a criminal. And I know that some women marry guys in prison so they must not all be ugly, but still! Come on, you guys! I think he's for real. He sounds English to me. Maybe he's just trying to seem American and that's why you don't think he sounds right, Carina. Maybe he is really rich, and so he doesn't know London the same way you do. He said his dad was a banker, after all. Then again, maybe you're jealous because you used to be the only foreign person around here. Everyone used to go on and on about how cute your accent is and now it's old. Everyone's used to you by now. How do we know you're telling the truth, Carina? For all we know, you're the fake around here.

(TEX *enters. When he sees* CARINA, *he starts to exit again.*)

CARINA: Tex?

TEX: Got to go find that math book.

CARINA: I was just telling the girls what a terrific blagger you are.

TEX: Oh. Thanks!

CARINA: You're a complete, ruddy blagger, aren't you?

TEX: Indubitably!

CARINA: You're a grotty, manky, naff yob who likes to snog midges!

TEX: Quite so! Well . . . the book . . .

(TEX exits.)

SHANNEN: What did you say?

CARINA: I said he was a dirty, idiotic, drunken slob who likes to French kiss tiny insects. So, do you believe me now?

Scene 2: Export

SHANNEN: Tex?

TEX: Yes, lovely lady?

SHANNEN: Can you come over here?

TEX: Certainly.

SHANNEN: I really love your accent. Where is it from again?

TEX: London, England.

SHANNEN: It's so cute! I'd love to know all about you, Tex: your childhood in England, the games you played, the foods you ate, the places you went . . .

TEX: My life has been dull. I'd rather talk about you.

SHANNEN: I've noticed that. Whenever I get you to try to talk about you, we always end up talking about me.

TEX: You are so much more fascinating.

SHANNEN: Oh, I doubt that. You seem very fascinating to me.

(MARY enters.)

MARY: Hello! Just the two people I wanted to see.

SHANNEN: Come on over, Mary! What's up?

MARY: Well, I've been reading about England. Specifically, London!

SHANNEN: How interesting! But why would you read up on London when you've got Tex here to tell you all about it?

MARY: What a splendid idea! Tex, will you tell me all about the Queen?

TEX: Certainly. She wears a crown and waves and wears hats.

SHANNEN: You know so much!

TEX: She's also old.

MARY: Fascinating!

SHANNEN: I was just telling him he's fascinating!

MARY: You're right, Shannen!

SHANNEN: I know, Mary!

MARY: Tex, I've been wondering about parliament. How does that work?

TEX: Well, a bunch of guys get together and yell at each other about making laws.

SHANNEN: What a colorful description! I feel like I'm right there!

MARY: Why do the judges and lawyers wear those wigs?

TEX: It started because way back when all the lawyers and judges were bald.

SHANNEN: Really!

MARY: How delightful!

SHANNEN: I was telling Tex before you arrived, Mary, that I'd like to know more about him.

MARY: Yes, Tex, tell us more!

TEX: Very well, what would you like to know?

SHANNEN: Do you have any brothers or sisters?

TEX: No, I'm afraid not.

(CARINA enters with DELL.)

CARINA: No? Then who's this?

DELL: (Speaking with a Southern accent.) What's with you, Tex?

TEX: I . . . I don't know who this young man is.

DELL: You sure as heck do.

TEX: Why, this young man's gone mad! Someone get him to a nurse.

CARINA: Don't you mean that we should get him to a wimperwolo?

TEX: Of course that's what I meant. I was speaking American.

CARINA: I made that word up.

TEX: Yes, yes. I thought you were just trying to joke around with the girls here.

DELL: Stop talking like that, you moron. You ashamed of your Southern roots or somethin'?

TEX: I am very proud of my Southern *English* roots!

CARINA: Give it up.

TEX: Give what up?

MARY: We went by your house the other day and met your brother, Dell.

SHANNEN: We asked him all about your English ancestry.

CARINA: Of course, he had no idea what we were talking about, *Tex.*

MARY: And, as you can see, he agreed to come to school with us today.

TEX: I've never met this man before in my life! *(Quietly to DELL.)* Will you shut up?

DELL: I've seen your face every day of my life, practically. You ain't no Englishman. You're a Texan. A redneck through and through. Nothin' to be ashamed of. I'm proud of what I am. So I don't know what all this messin' about is. You tryin' to mess with these girls? 'Cause that's not how our mama raised you, boy.

CARINA: Give it up, Tex. We've got you.

(Beat.)

TEX: *(Using a Texas accent.)* Fine. Fine! I'm from the South. I'm not English, never was. I don't know anything about tubes or wigs or anything.

CARINA: Did you actually think you'd get away with it?

TEX: Until I met you, yes!

DELL: Were you going to spend your whole life pretendin'?

TEX: Didn't think that far.

SHANNEN: So why did you do it?

TEX: Why did I do it? Isn't it obvious? People think English guys are smart. And all of you girls thought I was cute. If I were just myself, just dumb old Tex, would you've thought that? I doubt it. Moving to a whole new school in a whole new state, practically a world away, seemed like a huge opportunity to start a new life. Remake myself. I figured I could be anything and anyone I wanted. I couldn't change my name 'cause there would be records of that, but the rest I could tinker with. So I got to thinkin', what would I like to do? Who would I like to be? And I came to the conclusion that I wanted to charm the ladies and have everyone think I was real smart. So who can do that? It was then I started lookin' around me. Checkin' out what girls thought. Even sneaked a peek at some chick magazines. And I discovered girls like guys like Russell Crowe and Hugh Jackman. English guys. Accents. That gentleman stuff. So that's what I decided to be. And it worked! For a while, anyway.

CARINA: Russell Crowe and Hugh Jackman are Australian.

TEX: Close enough.

CARINA: England and Australia are practically on the other side of the world from one another.

TEX: Well, they both speak English with funny accents, OK?

MARY: But, Tex, I still don't get it. What's wrong with how you already are?

DELL: You said it, sweetie. These girls sure are a heck of a lot smarter than you, boy. You gotta be proud of who you are and where you come from. If you don't respect yourself, ain't no one gonna respect you. Am I right, y'all?

SHANNEN: So right.

DELL: You got to get out there and tell the world, "I am a good, clean Southern boy who likes fried steaks and apple pie. I like to fix cars and eat watermelons and go fishin'. I am a Texan, and I am an American!"

CARINA: Amen!

DELL: See me, girls? I like who I am. That's why I take good care of myself. I work out, see? Feel my biceps.

(CARINA, MARY, and SHANNEN immediately grab hold of his biceps.)

MARY: You're so strong!

DELL: I am strong, inside and out. I treat people right. I'm honest. That's what women want, Tex. Those English folks don't have nothin' on us. You got to love yourself, Tex, or ain't no one gonna love you.

SHANNEN: You said it, Dell!

DELL: It burns me up to think of you actin' like someone else. You straighten up, Tex, or I'm gonna tell Mama what you been doin'.

TEX: Aw, shut up, Dell. You're not the boss of me.

MARY: Don't be mean to Dell!

DELL: You keep it up, Tex. Just see if I don't.

(LINUS enters.)

CARINA: Come on, Dell. Let's not fight.

MARY: Maybe we should get out of here.

SHANNEN: We could go get some fried chicken!

DELL: You're lucky these girls know how much I like fried chicken, Tex. Otherwise, I'd give you a good talkin' to.

TEX: I'm shakin' in my boots, Dell.

CARINA: Let's go, Dell.

DELL: You girls sure are nice. I hope my brother didn't offend you.

MARY: You know, I forgot all about him.

SHANNEN: Did anyone ever tell you that you sound so cute?

DELL: Once or twice.

(DELL exits with MARY, SHANNEN, and CARINA trailing behind.)

LINUS: They sure like that Southern guy.

TEX: I guess.

LINUS: Maybe I should try talking with an accent.

TEX: I wouldn't recommend it. Or if you do, make sure you do a lot of research and hide your relatives first.

LINUS: Good idea. Maybe I'll try Italian. Spaghetti! Lasagna! Not bad, huh?

TEX: Keep workin' on it.

TALK BACK!

1. Do you have any assumptions about people with particular accents? If so, what are they?

2. What cultures seem exciting and exotic to you and why?

3. If you could remake yourself, what parts of your past and/or personality would you want to change?

4. Is Carina jealous of Tex or is she just concerned with truthfulness? Would you expose Tex's lie or would you keep your mouth shut?

5. Are there any parts of your regional or familial traditions that embarrass you? If so, why?

6. Are you interested in foreign cultures or do you feel more comfortable sticking with what you know? Is either inclination good or bad?

THE WARREN FAMILY

2F, 4M, 2V/O

WHO

FEMALES
Mollie
"Mrs. Warren"
Mrs. Warren (voiceover)

MALES
Josh
"Lester Warren"
Lester Warren
"Mr. Warren"
Mr. Warren (voiceover)

WHERE The Warren home.

WHEN Night.

🎭 If you're playing one of the actors, make sure you are very clear about when you're acting like one of the Warrens and when your character's "real" personality comes through.

✎ Invent for yourself the family and home you wish you had. Put yourself there, too. Write a scene and see how this new life and new family functions. Does it work? Where are the potential pitfalls?

Scene 1: Dinner

"LESTER": Could you please pass the butter, sister?

MOLLIE: Certainly, Lester. It would be my pleasure.

JOSH: Wow. You sure are polite.

"MRS.": How sweet of you to say so, Josh.

JOSH: I'm glad Mollie invited me over, Mrs. Warren. This meal is delicious.

"MR.": Your family has been so kind to Mollie, it's the least we could do.

MOLLIE: Seriously, Josh, your family is awesome.

JOSH: That's why I wanted to meet your family so much. I knew they'd be cool, too. You know Mollie seemed like she didn't want me to meet you guys for a while. I was starting to think you were ashamed of me, Mol.

MOLLIE: Ashamed of you? Don't be silly. I wasn't ashamed of you.

JOSH: What was it then? You couldn't be ashamed of your family, that's for sure. You guys are great.

"MR.": Thanks, son. We hope we'll be seeing a lot more of you.

MOLLIE: That's really nice, *Dad*, but Josh is really busy with school now. I don't think he'll be able to come over a lot.

JOSH: I'd love to! I am busy, but I can certainly clear my schedule if it means getting a great meal with good company.

"MRS.": Come over any time, Josh.

MOLLIE: Mom! Josh doesn't want to come here a lot.

"MRS.": I just want Josh to feel at home. Our home is your home, Josh!

JOSH: That's very generous of you.

MOLLIE: *Very* generous of you. Um, Josh, did Mom tell you that she and Dad are going to be going to China for a very, very long time soon? It's too bad because we'd love to have you over for dinner again, but since Mom's going to be gone for such a long time . . . I can't really cook, so . . .

"LESTER": How come I'm not going to China, too?

MOLLIE: You're too young. You go to school, remember?

JOSH: Lester, you're very bright for your age.

"LESTER": Thank you. I am rather precocious. At least that's what my professors tell me.

JOSH: Your professors?

MOLLIE: He means teachers. He goes to a weird school.

JOSH: Really. How old are you anyway, Lester?

"LESTER": I'm twelve.

JOSH: Twelve.

"LESTER": Yes. I think . . . Yes! Twelve.

MOLLIE: Yes, twelve.

JOSH: Wow. Your family must . . . Um, do you . . . shave?

MOLLIE: Ha ha ha ha ha! Lester is such a little scamp. When he was little he'd watch Dad shave, and he'd beg for Dad to let him shave, too. So, Dad gave in and so he's a twelve-year-old with whiskers! Funny, huh?

JOSH: Yeah. If I knew that worked, I'd have shaved at twelve, too.

"LESTER": I still appear quite young on camera. I've played as young as ten.

JOSH: Played?

MOLLIE: Ha, ha, ha, ha, ha! That's a good one. Lester—what a precocious kid!—he likes to make home movies.

"MRS.": Let's watch one!

MOLLIE: We can't.

"MR.": Why not, honey?

MOLLIE: We're eating.

"MRS.": Maybe when we're done eating then.

MOLLIE: But . . . the DVD player's broken, *remember*?

"MR.": Right, right. Lester broke it.

"LESTER": No, I didn't!

"MR.": I guess your mother broke it.

"MRS.": I'm sure I didn't.

"MR.": Then I guess I broke it.

"LESTER": You don't remember if you broke it? Maybe Mollie broke it.

"MR.": No, no. I remember now. I broke it. Silly me.

"MRS.": No home movies, I'm afraid!

JOSH: That's OK. So, what was Mollie like as a kid?

"MRS.": Oh, Mollie was so cute. So sweet. She really was the perfect child.

JOSH: Really? 'Cause she can have a temper sometimes.

MOLLIE: Josh!

JOSH: It's true!

"MRS.": Now that you mention it, Mollie once punched a hole in the wall behind you.

MOLLIE: No, I didn't.

"MRS.": Oh, honey, don't you remember? You were in a rage.

MOLLIE: No, I wasn't!

"LESTER": I remember that! She was angry at Aunt Agnes for bringing a fruitcake at Christmas. Fruitcakes are horrible, Josh.

JOSH: You punched a hole in the wall? How old were you?

MOLLIE: I didn't—

"MR.": Ten.

JOSH: She punched a hole in the wall when she was ten?

"MR.": Nine.

JOSH: Nine?

"MR.": Maybe she was eleven.

MOLLIE: I never punched a hole in the wall.

JOSH: Man, you were some angry kid. Strong, too! I don't think I could have done that. You must really hate fruitcake.

MOLLIE: It never happened! OK, everybody, *it never happened.*

"MRS.": Honey, just cool down.

"MR.": There's that rage again.

"LESTER": That's what she was like with Aunt Agnes.

MOLLIE: We don't even *have* an Aunt Agnes, OK?
Now let's get back to the approved topic list, please.

JOSH: You have a list?

MOLLIE: Well, not lit—

"LESTER": Yeah.

"MRS.": We've been having fine weather, haven't we?

JOSH: I think so. But I bet Mollie's been hating it, right,
Mol?

"MR.": Why is that, Molliekins?

JOSH: Mollie's the only girl I ever met who likes rainy
days better than sunny ones.

"LESTER": I guess that's why she's mad all the time.

MOLLIE: I'm not mad all the time!

"LESTER": Oh, right. I forgot. Um, Mollie's a really
great . . .

(Beat.)

"MRS.": Yes, Lester?

"LESTER": She's a really great . . .

(Beat.)

"MR.": Son?

"LESTER": Wait a minute. I'm thinking.

MOLLIE: Well, hurry up and finish thinking, Lester.

"LESTER": I forget. You made me forget.

JOSH: Maybe I should go. I have a lot of work to do. It's been great, though. I've really enjoyed myself.

MOLLIE: No, Josh, don't go. You haven't finished your dinner.

JOSH: I'm stuffed. It was delicious.

"LESTER": I remember now! Molly is a really great sister.

"MRS.": Lester, that's so sweet!

JOSH: Yeah, I gotta go. Thanks again.

(JOSH gets up from the table and crosses away from the table.)

MOLLIE: Wait!

(MOLLIE crosses to JOSH.)

MOLLIE: Why are you leaving? Aren't we having a nice time? I thought we were having a very nice time with my family. Doesn't my mother cook well? And she dresses very nicely, too. And my father is a successful businessman. Did you know that? He is very kind and supportive. My mother and I get along great. We're like best girl-friends, aren't we, Mom?

"MRS.": Um, yes, dear. I'm sure I agree with whatever you said.

MOLLIE: See? We are a happy, healthy, normal, loving family! So stay for dessert, Josh. We're having apple pie!

JOSH: I just never saw this side of you, Mollie.

MOLLIE: What side?

JOSH: You're acting different.

MOLLIE: Different? Me? Acting different? Why that is funny. That just makes me want to laugh, Josh! Don't be ridiculous. I'm being normal! Totally normal! Just like my family. Normal! Everything's fine here. We're going to have apple pie! Isn't that American?

JOSH: I really gotta go, Mol.

MOLLIE: Josh, please don't go! Please? I wanted this to be perfect. So you have to stay for dessert, please? We'll be better. We'll be whatever you want us to be. Just don't go yet!

JOSH: Can't you see how strange you're acting? All of you? I don't know what's going on exactly, but all of this is odd. Really. People don't act like this. Lester's trying to remember lines and shaving at twelve, Dad can't remember if he broke the DVD player or not and Mom—well, she's just so happy. Then there's you, raging at fruitcakes, trying to control everything. It's just weird. What am I supposed to think? You said "normal" about thirty times when you described your family a minute ago. You're making me think there are dead bodies buried in the basement or something.

MOLLIE: There's not!

JOSH: What am I supposed to think? I just—I don't know about this, Mollie. I really wanted to meet your family, but now . . . well, I'm sorry I did. No offense intended, but you're not exactly what I expected.

MOLLIE: What did you expect?

JOSH: I don't know any brothers and sisters who are so civil and polite with each other. At first, I thought it was nice, but you're taking this too far. You're just not genuine. I prefer people who are more honest, Mollie. Maybe . . . maybe we shouldn't see each other any more.

MOLLIE: No, Josh!

(LESTER enters.)

"MR.": We can take direction. Just tell us what you want.

LESTER: Excuse me.

JOSH: That's what I mean!

LESTER: Excuse me.

"MRS.": This is running long. Are we going to get paid for overtime?

LESTER: Excuse me!

(Beat. "MR.," "MRS.," "LESTER," JOSH, and MOLLIE all look at LESTER.)

LESTER: Who is everybody?

MOLLIE: Go away, little boy.

LESTER: Mollie, who is everybody?

"LESTER": Who are *you*?

LESTER: Lester.

"LESTER": You can't be Lester. I'm playing Lester!

Scene 2: Deserted

JOSH: You're both Lester?

MOLLIE: *(Putting her hands on LESTER's shoulders.)* This little boy is leaving now.

LESTER: I'm not a little boy.

MOLLIE: Bye-bye. You seem to be lost, stranger.

LESTER: I'm not a stranger. I'm your brother.

MOLLIE: Bye-bye! Don't you need to be somewhere, like a friend's house?

LESTER: I don't actually like Simon. And he doesn't actually like me. And I don't see why Mom and Dad let you stay at home and I had to go to Simon's house.

JOSH: So if you're Lester, who's this kid? *(Pointing at "Lester.")*

"LESTER": I'm Lester! You told me to be Lester.

MOLLIE: I didn't tell you anything.

JOSH: Did you hire this kid?

"LESTER": I better get paid or my Mom will be mad.

MOLLIE: Not if you don't shut up!

"LESTER": I'm going to tell my agent you said that!

LESTER: You're in my chair.

"LESTER": This is my mark. I'm supposed to sit here.

LESTER: Not any more.

"LESTER": So if you're so great, what movies have you been in?

LESTER: Movies are stupid. Only stupid people watch movies.

"LESTER": You're jealous.

LESTER: Of what? Your ugly face?

"LESTER": I'm adorable. Both my mother and my agent say so. And Danny DiVito said I was a pleasure to work with.

LESTER: Who's he?

"LESTER": He's famous.

LESTER: Never heard of him, doofus face.

MOLLIE: Oh, stranger? I think it's time you left now.

LESTER: I'm telling Mom and Dad you had a weird party while they were at the nudist camp.

(Beat.)

"MRS.": What a funny little boy.

LESTER: I'm not a little boy, horse-face lady!

MOLLIE: Lester!

JOSH: So he *is* Lester!

MOLLIE: I mean, strange kid—

JOSH: Give it up, Mollie. What's going on here?

LESTER: Yeah, what's going on here, buffalo butt?

MOLLIE: Shut up!

"MR.": Honey, I think your boyfriend wants to know what's going on. And to be honest, I'd like to know, too.

LESTER: Boyfriend? You have a boyfriend? Gross! Who'd kiss you?

MOLLIE: Shut up, maggot! I mean, kid . . . brother. OK, fine, everybody! This is my real brother. As my parents here know. I didn't want you to meet him, Josh, because as you can see, he is a little maggot. That's the whole story. That's why I didn't fight with this other kid. Because this kid is normal and my actual brother is not.

LESTER: Takes one to know one.

"LESTER": Can I go home now? I have to learn my lines. I play a precocious boy on a soap opera next week.

LESTER: You're old.

"LESTER": I look young on camera!

LESTER: You're eighty.

"LESTER": I'm . . . thirteen.

LESTER: More like thirty.

"LESTER": Fifteen, OK?

LESTER: You're short.

"LESTER": You're short.

LESTER: I'm twelve.

"LESTER": You stink.

LESTER: So? What's your point?

MOLLIE: Shut up, both of you! Now I hate you both.

"LESTER": I'm telling both my agent and my mother you said that.

MOLLIE: Oh, grow up. I know for a fact you're eighteen.

"LESTER": I'm calling my mom to pick me up.

MOLLIE: You drove here!

LESTER: I bet your feet don't touch the pedals.

"LESTER": Drop dead!

> (*"LESTER" exits.*)

"MRS.": Well. Why don't we settle down for dessert? We're having apple pie! Come on, everyone. Let's all take a breath and calm down.

LESTER: Don't tell me what to do.

"MRS.": Oh, Lester. You're such a delight. So very twelve.

LESTER: Who are you?

"MRS.": Ha, ha. I love it when we play this game. You tell me who I am, honey.

LESTER: You're nuts. You need medication.

MOLLIE: Maybe you should go now, Josh. You're so busy.

JOSH: I think I'll stay for dessert after all. I suspect this will be interesting.

("MRS." exits.)

"MR.": So, son, how was your day?

LESTER: None of your beeswax.

"MR.": Oh, pumpkin, that pie smells good!

"MRS.": I made it just for you, snookums!

("MRS." reenters with pie.)

LESTER: That's from the store. You didn't make that.

"MRS.": Of course I did, honey!

LESTER: Don't call me that. I don't know you.

MOLLIE: Lester, don't talk like that to Mom.

LESTER: Mom? Mom doesn't look anything like that. Mom has gray hair and walks around nak—

MOLLIE: I think the house is on fire! Everybody out! *(No one moves. MOLLIE becomes increasingly dramatic.)* Quickly! I smell something burning! It must be from the homemade pie! Quick! Go! Go! My God, we're going to die! All our cherished belongings ruined! How I've loved this house. Soon it will be nothing but ash! And our young lives will be snuffed out if we don't GET OUT OF THE HOUSE! Now!!!

(Beat. "MR.," "MRS.," LESTER, and JOSH all stare at MOLLIE.)

MOLLIE: Please? Go? Now? I . . . I thought I smelled something burning. I . . . guess maybe . . . I was wrong. So . . . we can go back to eating pie. Calmly and normally. Like we always do. Because that's how the Warren family is. Normal. Except for my funny brother Lester, who likes to tell funny stories. So, Lester, maybe you should stuff your mouth with pie. Lots and lots of pie. So you won't be talking, you'll be chewing your delicious pie that our lovely mother made for us. OK?

"MR.": I think I do smell something.

LESTER: We had burritos at Simon's house.

(*"MR." moves farther away from LESTER.*)

"MR.": Son, take it easy on the burritos.

"MRS.": Why don't we give you some pie, like Mollie suggested?

LESTER: I don't like pie from the store. And you're not my mother.

MOLLIE: He's adopted. It explains his rude behavior.

LESTER: I'm not adopted. You're adopted.

MOLLIE: No, you are.

LESTER: Mom and Dad said you were.

MOLLIE: You wish.

LESTER: Yeah, I do. So when are they back from their gross vacation?

"MRS.": We're taking off work until next week.

LESTER: Good for you. So answer my question, Mollie Moron.

MOLLIE: I don't know what you're talking about.

JOSH: Mollie, it's so obvious. These people are not your parents. They're actors you hired or something. I guess your parents are nudists so you didn't want me to meet them. I can understand

that. But . . . they must put on clothes sometimes, right? Like maybe to meet their daugh-
ter's boyfriend?

LESTER: So do you kiss her dogface?

MOLLIE: Shut up, Lester.

JOSH: See? Now this is how brothers and sisters
are supposed to act. You're supposed to fight.
I fight with my sister all the time.

MOLLIE: You do? You didn't when I was there.

JOSH: If you didn't see us fight, you must have been
to my house on a good day.

MOLLIE: But your family is normal.

JOSH: You shouldn't be ashamed of your family,
Mollie. All families are abnormal. It's normal to
be abnormal. My dad, every night, tells a joke
about a rabbi, a priest, and a carpenter. Every
night. The same exact joke. And he laughs every
time. My sister talks on the phone twenty-four
seven about some guy named Chad and listens to
hip-hop. She thinks she's street. It's sad. My
mom? Well . . . She calls me . . . poopsie puppy.
It's a name from when I was a baby. It's embarrassing. So there you go. We all have things to
be embarrassed by.

MOLLIE: But your parents wear clothes.

JOSH: True. But don't they dress for company?

MOLLIE: I don't know.

JOSH: Don't they ever leave the house?

MOLLIE: Well, maybe. I hope so.

JOSH: Can't you just ask?

MOLLIE: I guess so.

JOSH: Trust me a little. I can't imagine your real family could be stranger than your pretend family.

MOLLIE: Well . . . I don't know about that.

JOSH: At least they'll be real. I've already met the real Lester here, and I get him. He's a smart-ass. But it's OK. I don't mind.

LESTER: You think you know everything.

JOSH: I like you, Mollie.

MOLLIE: I like you, too, Josh.

JOSH: So when am I going to meet your real family?

MOLLIE: Someday—

MRS.: *(Voiceover from offstage.)* I can't wait to get these clothes off!

MR.: Me, too, honey! Let's get comfortable!

(Beat.)

MOLLIE: Everyone. Out. Now!

TALK BACK!

1. What's a "normal" family?

2. If you could swap any of your family members for an actor, who would it be and why?

3. What makes a person secretive about his or her life?

4. Often, we speak of politicians and public figures having "skeletons in [their] closets." Does everyone have these or can they be avoided?

5. What would you do if you found out your boyfriend/girlfriend/best friend had a really unusual family? Would it affect your relationship?

6. Do you consider yourself open or judgmental? Are there any lifestyles or beliefs that are unacceptable to you? If so, what makes them unacceptable?

HIGH SCHOOL BOYFRIEND

2F, 2M

WHO

FEMALES	MALES
Mina	Hart
Suvi	Logan

WHERE Scene 1: At the mall's food court; Scene 2: At Suvi's house.

WHEN Scene 1: Afternoon; Scene 2: Evening.

🎭 Make the conversation as light and natural as possible. In rehearsal, try underplaying it by sitting very close to the other actors (so you don't need to project). When you get up to perform onstage, see if you can keep the same relaxed quality while sending the performance outward.

✎ Here's your theme: The World's Worst Breakup. Write a play based on this subject. Make it as disaster-filled as possible. Enjoy making your characters suffer for the audience's entertainment!

Scene 1: Buh-Bye

MINA: So, we're going to college soon.

HART: Right!

MINA: In different states.

HART: Right!

MINA: Soon.

HART: Right!

MINA: So maybe we should see less of each other.

HART: Don't worry. I'll be sure to make time for you when I'm not packing.

MINA: Uh, thanks. But you don't have to.

HART: Sure I do! You're my girlfriend. Don't get worried. I said I'd be there for you and I meant it. You won't be able to get rid of me!

MINA: Great!

HART: *(Singing.)* "No matter the distance / I want you to know / That deep down inside of me—"

MINA: Don't sing.

HART: You like my singing!

MINA: Not in public.

HART: Right. That's just our private song.

MINA: Actually, I don't really like that song.

HART: You're so funny, Mina! That's one of my favorite things about you.

MINA: I'm not funny at all. Actually, I hate the way I have a total lack of humor. I'm humorless. I'm like the black hole of humor. I'm where laughter goes to die.

HART: Hysterical! You kill me.

MINA: I wish.

HART: See? You slay me.

MINA: If only.

HART: Do you want another soda?

MINA: If I have any more soda, I'll get gas.

HART: You know you're really close to someone when you can talk about gas together.

MINA: You think so?

HART: Definitely!

MINA: I always thought that was the sign that the fire was gone. That things were over, kaput, dead and buried.

HART: No. Not at all! It just means we're comfortable. That we can really communicate and share.

MINA: Have you been watching *Oprah* or something?

HART: It's summer! I have seen an *Oprah* or two. It helps me understand the female mind.

MINA: I prefer my men to be men.

HART: Don't worry. I watch NASCAR all weekend long. I'm all man!

MINA: I hate cars.

HART: That's why you need a boyfriend like me. Or else what would you do if you needed an oil change?

MINA: I'd take my car to a garage.

HART: But you don't have to! Because you have me, baby.

MINA: Fan-freakin'-tastic.

HART: You said it. Hey, I'm going to get another drink. You sure you don't want one?

MINA: I'm absolutely sure.

HART: Are you sure? You love Diet Coke.

MINA: I hate Diet Coke.

HART: Right! As if I don't know you drink it all the time! So . . . should I get you one?

MINA: No!

HART: OK! Be back in a minute . . . Don't miss me too much!

(*HART exits. MINA pulls out a phone.*)

MINA: Suvi, get over here now! I need to be saved.

(*MINA puts her phone away. HART returns.*)

HART: I got you a Diet Coke anyway, just in case you changed your mind.

MINA: But I told you I didn't want a Diet Coke.

HART: Right. But sometimes you say you don't want something, then you change your mind. Like remember that time when I ordered dessert and you said you didn't want one, and then you ate like half of my hot fudge sundae?

MINA: I remember that it was a couple of months ago.

HART: A couple. You know, every time I hear that word I think of you. Isn't that weird? I never thought I'd be like that. But we are just so perfect together, aren't we? I'm sure gonna miss you in college. But we're going to visit each other every weekend, right?

MINA: About that, I just don't have that kind of money. I don't think it would be possible.

HART: I've got a surprise for you.

MINA: What?

HART: Know how I've been working after school all year?

MINA: Yeah.

HART: The job I got through my dad's friend—remember?

MINA: Right.

HART: Well, I never told you, but they paid me a lot, and I got overtime, too, for working a few hours extra every day. I made enough money so I can visit you as much as I want!

MINA: You're kidding.

HART: No! Plus, my parents love you, so I'm sure that if I run out of cash they would lend some to me so I can see you. They'd be happy to have me back home, and I could stay with them and come visit you—it will be just like old times! It will be like college never even started and we're still in high school.

MINA: But, Hart, I want to go to college.

HART: Of course you'll go to college, Mina, I don't mean that. I mean that it will just socially seem like high school still. Just us hanging out together doing the same old stuff.

MINA: I'd like to do some new stuff.

HART: We can do new stuff, too! We can do whatever you want.

(SUVI enters.)

SUVI: I came as soon as I could, Mina.

HART: Hi, Suvi! What are you doing here?

MINA: I asked her to come.

HART: How come?

MINA: I want to spend time with all my friends before we split up to go to college. Before we all *split up* to go to college.

HART: You repeated yourself.

MINA: Did I? I guess my mind must be *splitting up*.

HART: Don't you mean "cracking up"?

MINA: I think I meant SPLITTING UP.

HART: I think your mind's split up.

MINA: It's good to split up sometimes.

HART: Hey, Suvi, want a soda? I'm rolling in it.

SUVI: Nah.

MINA: Sure you do!

SUVI: I'm fine.

MINA: Suvi, don't offend Hart! He's offering you a soda!

SUVI: OK, OK! I'll have a Diet Coke.

HART: What is it with girls and Diet Coke?

SUVI: It has no calories.

MINA: I guess we'll have to *split up* for a while, while you get that Diet Coke.

HART: But she can have the one I bought you, since you don't want it.

MINA: I want it now.

HART: See! I told you so. Be back soon!

(HART exits.)

SUVI: What is wrong with you?

MINA: He will not take a hint, Suvi! I've been trying to break up with him all afternoon!

SUVI: Why do you want to break up with him anyway? You've been such a tight couple for so long.

MINA: That's just it. We've been together too long. It's time for us to move on. We're going to college soon. College! It's a chance to meet new people, try new things, make new friends . . . I would really like some of those new people, things, and friends to be cute college guys.

SUVI: It just seems like you've turned off Hart so quickly.

MINA: I know! It's true. And **I feel bad about how** I'm acting now. But all of sudden everything I used to love about him is really annoying me. I used to think it was cute that he sort of badgered me into ordering things in restaurants. It made me feel like a princess. Now I just think, "No, for the ten billionth time, I do *not* want another order of French fries!" Why can't he take no for an answer? Why can't he break up with me? I've disagreed with everything he's said all day. He thinks it's *funny*, Suki! What am I supposed to do? I don't want to hurt his feelings. I would really like *him* to break up with *me*, but he won't! I think he actually believes that we're going to be together forever.

SUVI: That's romantic.

MINA: I'm embarrassed to say I actually thought that myself for a while. But we're *young*. I've got my whole life ahead of me. No way am I going to end up with my high school boyfriend! There's a big world out there just waiting for me. It's bad enough I have to go to college near home, there's just no way I'm going to keep living my same old, boring, high school life!

SUVI: Thanks a lot.

MINA: I didn't mean you were old and boring. You know what I mean.

SUVI: **Know what I think?**

MINA: No.

SUVI: I think you're crazy. Spoiled beyond belief. You have this great guy who just wants to do nice things for you, spend time with you, spend his money on you, give you attention and love, and you're ungrateful. I would love that! Every girl would! Hart treats you like a goddess. And you're just trying to find the next best thing! What if there isn't anyone better? Have you thought about that? And you've treated him so badly? Maybe one day you'll be one of those women on talk shows who's dying to meet her first love, her high school sweetheart, because now she realizes that he's the best guy she ever knew. So then they bring him out and—guess what!—he's married with three kids. You blew it. Or, he hates you and never wants to see you again. You'd deserve that, Mina, because you take Hart for granted. If there were an award for World's Best Boyfriend, he would win it. You're crazy if you let him go.

MINA: I guess I'm crazy then.

(HART enters.)

MINA: Shhh!

HART: Talking about girl stuff? Here's your Diet Coke, Suvi. I got you a cookie, too.

SUVI: Why?

HART: I just thought you might want one.

SUVI: I'm on a diet. Hence the Diet Coke.

HART: You look fine.

SUVI: Well, thanks, I guess.

HART: Besides, I bet Mina will help you polish it off. Once she ate my hot fudge sundae—

MINA: We need to split up.

HART: Oh, I forgot to get a knife so you can split up the cookie! I'll be back!

MINA: Do you see what I mean?

SUVI: I guess so.

MINA: Help me!

SUVI: I'll try.

Scene 2: Hello

HART: Do you want me to get you something to drink?

MINA: OK, but be back in five minutes.

HART: OK.

MINA: Five minutes!

HART: I'll be back, don't worry!

(HART exits. SUVI enters.)

MINA: Suvi!

SUVI: There you are! Great party, huh?

MINA: Yeah, yeah. So where's your cousin?

SUVI: He's coming.

MINA: He needs to be here now! Let's get this over with before I kill Hart.

SUVI: Calm down, Mina.

MINA: If this doesn't work, I don't know what I'll do. I guess I'll have to marry him and have his babies and live happily ever after, dammit!

SUVI: Seriously, calm down. It's going to work. No way will Hart still want to go out with you if he sees you kissing another guy.

MINA: And you swear that your cousin is (A) not ugly,

(B) understands the plan, and (C) isn't going to stick his tongue down my throat?

SUVI: Logan gets it. He's fine with it. He thinks it's funny. He's a nice guy. You'll like him.

MINA: So where is he? Hart's going to be back any minute! I thought he was going to be here!

SUVI: He is here. Somewhere. He told me he'd make his way over here. Hold on. I'll find him.

(SUVI scans the "crowd." LOGAN enters.)

SUVI: Logan! Logan!

(LOGAN sees SUVI and begins to walk over to her.)

MINA: He is cute!

SUVI: Told you.

MINA: I don't think you're supposed to know your cousin is cute.

SUVI: Shut up.

LOGAN: Hi. I guess you're Mina.

MINA: Right.

LOGAN: Great! I was worried you'd be ugly and I wouldn't want to stick my tongue down your throat.

(Beat as MINA looks shocked.)

LOGAN: Just kidding. So, should we get to it?

MINA: Sure.

LOGAN: OK.

(LOGAN moves closer to MINA. SUVI still stands between the two of them.)

LOGAN: Um, Suvi?

SUVI: Yes?

LOGAN: This might be a little less awkward without you standing here watching.

SUVI: Oh. OK!

(SUVI exits.)

LOGAN: So, Mina, how come you want to get rid of this guy so badly? I mean, what could he have done that was so bad that you'd want to treat him like this?

MINA: Well, I'm going to college, and he's my high school boyfriend, know what I mean?

LOGAN: Unfortunately, I know exactly what you mean. This is pretty much what my high school girlfriend did to me. I was thinking everything was fine, then zap! She told me she wanted to break up so she could see college guys. I was totally torn up. So I know what your boyfriend is going to go through. It isn't very nice. Especially if there isn't any warning. It really hurts.

MINA: Are you serious? Well, I'm sorry. I mean, I don't want to hurt anyone—

LOGAN: I have to give my ex some credit, though. At least she just came out and told me she wanted to break up. She didn't stage a whole scene. Why don't you just tell your boyfriend how you feel instead of coming up with a whole dramatic plot to get rid of him?

MINA: But that's just it! I've told him a hundred times that I want to break up. He won't take the hint! Honestly, I would rather he broke up with me. I hinted, I cajoled, I argued, and I even begged. He won't listen. Then I just told him. We're through. It's over. He laughed, Logan! He thought it was a joke. I'm taking these extreme measures because I don't know what else to do! Can't you understand? If you have any other suggestions, I am open to them. Really.

LOGAN: Well, that's what Suvi told me. I guess I understand why you're doing this. I guess I just needed to hear it for myself. Part of me just feels sorry for this guy, you know?

MINA: I know.

LOGAN: But, to be honest, another part of me really wants to kiss you.

MINA: Oh! Well . . . great.

LOGAN: So . . .

(LOGAN leans in.)

MINA: So! You go to college!

LOGAN: Yes. I go to college. I'm going to be a sophomore next year.

(LOGAN leans in.)

MINA: Where do you go to school?

LOGAN: I go to USC.

MINA: That's where I'm going to go!

LOGAN: That's great. Maybe we'll see each other there.

MINA: That would be nice.

(LOGAN leans in. He takes MINA's face in his hands and looks deeply into her eyes as HART re-enters with drinks.)

HART: Did you get something in your eye again?

MINA: What? No. We were . . . we were going to kiss, Hart. I'm sorry you caught us. I feel terrible.

HART: Right! Hi, I'm Hart.

LOGAN: Um, I'm Logan.

HART: Hey, thanks for helping with the eye thing. I can take it from here, buddy.

MINA: But we were going to kiss.

HART: Right.

MINA: You don't believe me?

HART: No, I believe you.

MINA: Then . . . I'm confused.

HART: I've been wanting to tell you. I think we should see other people.

MINA: You do?

HART: I don't want to hurt you or anything, but . . . we're going off to college. We're bound to meet other people and it's only natural that we'll want to . . . explore other options. It's hard having a long-distance relationship. We're used to being together all the time. Spending every minute together. And I'm a guy who really likes to be with people. I'm a people person. But we can still see each other! It just won't be exclusive anymore. But I still plan on coming down on weekends to visit. We have a lot of fun, right? Why ruin that? I'm just saying, let's take it easy. It's not like we're ready to get married. We're young! We should live life to it's fullest. That's what I always say. Or, at least, I'm going to start saying that. And if you want to just see me, that's OK. I'm just saying, I'd like to open things up a bit. Can you understand that?

MINA: No.

HART/LOGAN: What?

MINA: No!

HART: Why not?

MINA: Because I am not going to see other people *and* see you. And you shouldn't do that either! You should see one person. Otherwise, it's cheating.

HART: I didn't think you'd be like this. I thought our relationship was strong enough—

MINA: It's not. We need to just break up.

(*Beat while HART thinks.*)

HART: That's how you really feel?

MINA: Yes!

(*Beat while HART thinks.*)

HART: Well, then. I'll break up with Suvi.

MINA: What?

HART: Well, Suvi and I were talking the other night and one thing led to another . . .

MINA: Suvi! Are you serious? I hate you both!

HART: But I'm going to break up with her! I just thought that you've seemed unhappy lately, maybe you wanted to cool off a little.

MINA: Suvi and you?

HART: We're through. Don't be mad, Mina. It's just you and me from here on out.

(Beat as MINA thinks.)

MINA: So you and Suvi are through?

HART: If that's what you want, that's what you'll get.

MINA: Well . . . that's what I want.

LOGAN: What?

HART: Done.

MINA: Get me a Diet Coke, Hart.

HART: Anything you want.

MINA: And some cake.

HART: Be right back.

(HART exits.)

LOGAN: But I thought—

MINA: You can go away now.

LOGAN: OK. This was really confusing.

MINA: You're telling me.

TALK BACK!

1. Are you the kind of person who likes to be with just one person or prefers to "play the field"? Why?

2. Is Mina's plan with Logan fair? Why or why not?

3. Who's worse—Hart or Mina? Which one is more deceptive?

4. What do you look for in a boyfriend or girlfriend? What are the ten most important qualities?

5. What's the best way to break up with someone?

6. Is dating more than one person cheating if you're not married?

7. What makes a habit change from charming to annoying (like Hart's habit of buying things Mina doesn't want)? What qualities would you be unwilling to overlook in a potential love interest?

BARBIE GOES TO HIGH SCHOOL

5F, 5M

WHO

FEMALES	MALES
Barbie	Alan
Jacinta	Chaz
Rachel	Ken
Dawn	Kent
Mimi	Matt

WHERE Scene 1: The school gym; Scene 2: The school cafeteria.

WHEN Present day.

🎭 The key with slapstick (physically based comedy) is to be very specific and sharp with your movements. Your timing also has to be precise.

🖎 Take another character from pop culture or fiction and put him or her into a normal, present-day situation. What problems would this character face in the real world? What might he or she be especially good at that is unexpected? See what comic discoveries you can make.

Scene 1: Girl Time

(BARBIE is smiling. BARBIE always smiles.)

RACHEL: So you're new.

BARBIE: You bet!

RACHEL: I hate P.E.

BARBIE: I like it.

RACHEL: You do?

BARBIE: I do!

RACHEL: Do you like dodge ball?

BARBIE: I like dodge ball.

RACHEL: Why do they make us play this? It's like a game for four-year-olds.

BARBIE: It's fun. I like fun.

(DAWN and JACINTA enter.)

DAWN: Don't just stand there!

JACINTA: Try to catch the balls. Then they're out automatically.

BARBIE: OK!

(DAWN and JACINTA exit. A ball rolls across the stage.)

DAWN: *(From offstage.)* Get the ball!

(RACHEL stands still.)

RACHEL: I hate P.E.

(BARBIE cannot bend her knees or elbows. She awkwardly walks over to the ball, bends at the waist and tries to pick it up. Her hands won't come close enough together to pick it up. BARBIE tries anyway. Through all this, RACHEL watches BARBIE curiously.)

RACHEL: No offense, but are you handicapped?

BARBIE: No, why?

RACHEL: I don't know. I just thought . . .

BARBIE: I like the handicapped.

RACHEL: Everybody likes the handicapped.

(JACINTA enters.)

JACINTA: Why didn't you pick up the ball?

BARBIE: I can't reach it.

(The ball is at BARBIE's feet.)

JACINTA: Whatever!

(JACINTA quickly snatches up the ball and exits.)

RACHEL: This is stupid. Who thought of this any-way? This is like a school-sanctioned way for people to beat up the nerdy kids. It's torture. Do you know that I had a circle-shaped bruise on my thigh all through first grade? It never went away. I was almost relieved on the days when they'd make us do square dancing with the boys. And we all know how awful square dancing is.

BARBIE: I like square dancing.

RACHEL: Oh. Sorry. I didn't know anyone liked square dancing. I was just about to say that I can't believe they still make kids do that kind of stuff since no one's been into square dancing for real in, like, forever. But maybe I was wrong. It was probably fine for you since you're the sort of girl boys don't pick on. Sure, they'll probably pull your hair from time to time, but only to get your attention 'cause they like you. They called me Booger until I was ten because *once* I *scratched* my nose in kindergarten. No one tells you that one little mistake is going to cost you for the rest of your life, right? And I swear I was just scratching. Boys suck.

BARBIE: I like boys.

DAWN: *(From offstage.)* Catch it!

(A ball lightly bounces toward BARBIE. She reaches out to catch it, and it flies between her arms and hits her.)

RACHEL: Are you OK?

BARBIE: I feel great!

RACHEL: You're out, I guess.

BARBIE: That's OK.

(BARBIE starts to exit. JACINTA and DAWN enter.)

DAWN: What's wrong with you?

RACHEL: You guys—

JACINTA: You could have caught that.

RACHEL: You guys—

DAWN: We're going to lose because of you.

RACHEL: You guys! I don't think she can catch.

JACINTA: Well, duh. That's obvious.

RACHEL: You guys!

(RACHEL indicates for DAWN and JACINTA to walk over to her. They do.)

DAWN: What?

RACHEL: You guys, I don't think she can put her arms together.

JACINTA: Maybe her boobs are in the way.

RACHEL: No really. I think she has a problem. So be nice.

DAWN: Oh great. Another pathetic freak on our team.

RACHEL: Why are you so competitive?

JACINTA: Why do you ask dumb questions?

(MIMI enters.)

MIMI: Hi! I'm Mimi. I guess you're out now.

BARBIE: No, I'm Barbie.

MIMI: You are so funny! Come sit with me. I can tell you all the gossip about everyone in school. By the way, your outfit today is so cute. I noticed it right away.

BARBIE: I have seventy-two different coordinating outfits. There's the cowgirl one and the going-to-the-beach one—

MIMI: Where are you from? I love you!

BARBIE: I'm from Malibu.

MIMI: California? Oh my God. No wonder you're so cool.

BARBIE: Thanks!

MIMI: We should hang out sometimes.

BARBIE: We could drive somewhere in my pink car.

MIMI: Your car is pink? Oh my God! That's awesome!

DAWN: I think we're in an alternate universe.

JACINTA: Let's get back into the game. Forget these losers.

MIMI: Um, excuse me Ms. Sweaty Jocks, but I don't think we're the losers.

DAWN: Whatever.

(DAWN and JACINTA exit.)

MIMI: So you're wearing heels in gym class. That is dedication.

BARBIE: My feet don't go flat.

RACHEL: But don't they hurt?

BARBIE: No.

RACHEL: I can't wear heels at all. I fall over.

MIMI: I'm not surprised.

RACHEL: What is that supposed to mean?

(A ball hits RACHEL in the back.)

RACHEL: Ow!

BARBIE: I guess we're all out then.

MIMI: *(To BARBIE.)* Let's go gossip.

BARBIE: OK!

JACINTA: *(From offstage.)* Get the ball!

(MIMI, BARBIE, and RACHEL head for the wall, ignoring the ball.)

DAWN: *(From offstage.)* Losers!

MIMI: Ew. Jocks are so rude. I could never be like that, you know? What's the point? Best possible scenario? You win a stupid game in gym class. Who cares? I just can't take it that seriously, you know? I mean a person could hurt herself doing this stuff. You could get broken bones or bruises. I personally avoid pain. This makes sense to me. Who wants pain? Who wants some yucky bruises? And if you break your bones your body, like, atrophies under the cast! I had this friend, right, and she broke her leg in, like, fourth grade, and when the cast was taken off, her left leg—the one that broke—was, like, half the size of the other leg. Ew! Am I right? Who wants that? And I am not a competitive person besides. We're all sisters, right? Why should we compete against each other?

RACHEL: You're a feminist?

MIMI: Ew, no! I'm not a feminist. Those people don't shave their legs or anything. Gross. Why am I talking to you? *(To BARBIE.)* I know we're going to be friends. As long as you stay away from my boyfriend, Matt.

RACHEL: Oh, you're not competitive.

MIMI: You know, people would like you better if you were a little nicer.

RACHEL: I am nice. Aren't I nice?

BARBIE: She's nice.

MIMI: Yeah. You probably shouldn't talk to her anymore. *(To RACHEL.)* No offense.

RACHEL: Why would that offend me? And you say *I'm* not nice.

MIMI: I'm just being honest.

RACHEL: And this is why we won't ever get along. When you're mean you call it honest. When I'm honest you call it mean.

MIMI: No, I'd probably call it jealousy.

RACHEL: I wouldn't want to be you, though. I know you think I do, but I don't. I like being smart.

MIMI: And you wouldn't want a boyfriend and popularity.

RACHEL: I wouldn't want your boyfriend, no offense, and I don't care about being popular.

MIMI: Right.

RACHEL: Right!

BARBIE: So everybody agrees! You guys are great.

We're going to have so much fun, I can tell. We can go to the beach and go to nightclubs—

RACHEL: We're in Ohio. There are no beaches.

MIMI: And no nightclubs.

BARBIE: Oh, well, we'll just have to go to a lot of movie premieres.

RACHEL: Barbie, you're not in Malibu anymore.

Scene 2: Boy Time

(MIMI, MATT, KEN, and CHAZ sit at a table. BARBIE walks onstage holding a lunch tray at arms' length. She cannot bend her arms or legs. She looks for a place to sit. MIMI stands and crosses to BARBIE.)

MIMI: Barbie!

(BARBIE turns and hits MIMI with the tray.)

MIMI: Ouch!

BARBIE: I'm so sorry!

MIMI: It's OK. Come sit down with us!

(BARBIE walks over to the table and puts down her tray. With difficulty, she sits down.)

MIMI: You guys, this is the girl I was telling you about. This is Barbie!

MATT: Hey.

KEN: Hey.

CHAZ: What up?

BARBIE: Hi! Thanks for letting me sit with you.

MIMI: I've been telling these guys about how cool you are.

BARBIE: Thanks! You're cool, too.

MIMI: Thanks! We have so much in common.

BARBIE: We do?

MIMI: Sure! I like pink, too.

BARBIE: Oh my goodness! You're right.

MIMI: See? So, Barbie, these are The Guys—Matt, my boyfriend; Ken; and Chaz. Say hi to Barbie, you guys!

MATT: Hey.

KEN: Hey.

CHAZ: What up?

MIMI: So isn't Barbie totally cute?

KEN: Yeah, you are pretty cute.

MATT: Yeah.

MIMI: Matt! I'm right *here*. That is so wrong.

MATT: You asked.

MIMI: Not you.

MATT: Oh.

CHAZ: So, you're new?

BARBIE: Yeah.

MIMI: Matt, stop looking at her!

MATT: She's talking!

MIMI: It's the way you're looking at her.

MATT: With my eyes?

BARBIE: I had a boyfriend named Ken.

KEN: Oh yeah?

BARBIE: Yeah.

KEN: What happened?

BARBIE: His head came off.

MIMI: Oh my God! I'm so sorry.

BARBIE: They put it back on.

CHAZ: They did?

BARBIE: Yeah, but he was never the same.

MIMI: I'm so sorry.

BARBIE: It's OK.

> (Beat. MATT, CHAZ, KEN, and MIMI eat. BARBIE
> manages to grasp her water bottle with her arm fully
> extended. Lifting her arm above her head, she tries
> to pour some water into her mouth. It spills on her
> shirt and face.)

MIMI: Oh my God! You spilled your drink all over you.

BARBIE: Whoops. I'll go get a napkin.

(BARBIE tries to stand. ALAN enters.)

BARBIE: Oh, young man?

ALAN: Who me?

BARBIE: Would you get me a napkin?

ALAN: Uh . . . uh . . . uh . . .

BARBIE: Please?

(ALAN stares and stutters.)

KEN: Go on, moron!

(KEN stands and pushes ALAN offstage.)

BARBIE: Thank you, Ken.

KEN: No problem, Barbie.

MIMI: Maybe you should put something else on.

BARBIE: It's OK. It will dry.

MIMI: You did it on purpose, didn't you?

BARBIE: What?

MIMI: Made your shirt all wet.

BARBIE: No. It was an accident.

MIMI: You want to steal my boyfriend, don't you?

BARBIE: No. I want my own boyfriend.

(ALAN *enters with a napkin. He holds it out to* BARBIE.)

BARBIE: Thank you.

ALAN: Uh . . . uh . . .

KEN: You can go now.

ALAN: Uh . . .

(KEN *pushes* ALAN *offstage.*)

ALAN: *(From offstage.)* You're welcome!

BARBIE: What a nice boy. (BARBIE *holds the napkin, perplexed about what to do with it. Everyone stares.*) I wish Ken were here.

CHAZ: So Barbie, what are you doing Friday night?

KEN: I was just going to ask the same thing.

MATT: Me, too. I mean, I was wondering for you guys. Because I have a girlfriend. A really great, understanding girlfriend.

MIMI: Barbie, maybe you should sit at another table.

BARBIE: What? Why?

MIMI: I don't think we can be friends after all.

BARBIE: Why?

MIMI: I think you're too slutty for me.

BARBIE: What?

MIMI: You're trying to steal my boyfriend.

BARBIE: No, I'm not.

MIMI: Yes, you are.

BARBIE: No. Really.

KEN: Calm down, Mimi. Maybe Barbie doesn't like Matt. Maybe she likes someone else.

CHAZ: Yeah. What are you looking for, Barbie?

BARBIE: I like boys named Ken.

KEN: Ha!

BARBIE: I like boys.

CHAZ: Ha!

BARBIE: I like boys who are clean cut and nice.

MATT: Ha!

(MATT pretends to choke to cover up his error.)

MIMI: Matt! Barbie, I think you should leave now.

(ALAN enters as BARBIE tries to stand up without bending her arms or legs.)

BARBIE: Young man, would you help me move to another table?

ALAN: Uh . . .

CHAZ: I'll help you.

KEN: Not if I beat you to it.

(KEN and CHAZ both stand and rush to BARBIE's aid. Both boys pull her upright then tug her back and forth between them.)

CHAZ: I said I would help her!

KEN: I said I would!

MIMI: You guys are pathetic! Come on, Matt.

MATT: What?

MIMI: Come on, Matt. We're leaving.

MATT: Oh. Are you sure?

MIMI: Yes!

MATT: Oh. OK.

(MATT and MIMI exit.)

CHAZ: Well, I guess you didn't have to move after all.

ALAN: Uh.

KEN: Why don't we sit down and have a nice, quiet lunch now? Just the two of us?

CHAZ: You wish, Ken. Maybe Barbie likes her men more smooth. Would you like anything, Barbie?

KEN: If you need anything, you can ask me.

CHAZ: Back off, Ken! Don't mind him.

KEN: She likes Kens, remember?

CHAZ: You look thirsty.

KEN: I'll get you something to drink.

CHAZ: I will!

(KEN and CHAZ put BARBIE down and both run to get BARBIE a drink.)

ALAN: Uh . . . here. *(Gets his nerve up; wipes off BARBIE's face.)*

BARBIE: Thank you!

(BARBIE smiles warmly at ALAN. ALAN passes out. MATT enters and steps over ALAN's body to sit beside BARBIE.)

MATT: Hi, Barbie.

BARBIE: Hi.

MATT: So. Never mind about Mimi. She's gone a little nuts. We have an open relationship, actually. We can see anyone we want. So I'm actually free to date any girl in school. And I really thought we hit it off, Barbie. So . . . do you want to go out sometime? Like maybe Friday night?

BARBIE: That will make Mimi mad.

MATT: Don't worry about Mimi. What do you think, Barbie? Because I'd really like to take you out. I think we could have a really excellent time. We could go someplace nice and quiet for dinner, maybe catch a movie. I could show you around town. Be your tour guide.

BARBIE: Oh. That would be nice. But—

MATT: No buts. Let me show you a good time, Barbie. Just some conversation. See how things go.

(MIMI enters.)

BARBIE: Mimi—

MATT: Mimi, schmimi. Don't worry about her. She's actually very open-minded.

MIMI: Am I?

MATT: Mimi? No. I meant—I was paying you a compliment. Telling Barbie what a great girl you are and how we're so into each other.

MIMI: I told you not to talk to her!

MATT: You can't tell me what to do.

MIMI: I can and I will tell you what to do! Because you're my boyfriend and that's my job and my prerogative. It's the rules. I get to tell you what to do, so get used to it!

(KENT enters. He holds his tray out in front of him and walks without bending his knees, as BARBIE does.)

KENT: Is anyone sitting here?

MIMI: We're leaving!

MATT: Well—

MIMI: WE'RE LEAVING!

MATT: Right. Later, Barbie.

(MIMI yanks MATT offstage.)

KENT: May I?

BARBIE: Sure!

(KENT sits down across from BARBIE with difficulty.)

KENT: It's my first day here.

BARBIE: Me, too!

KENT: I like it.

BARBIE: Me, too!

KENT: But I'm not sure anyone likes me.

BARBIE: Me, too. *(Beat.)* What's your name?

KENT: Kent.

BARBIE: Oh.

KENT: What's your name?

BARBIE: Barbie.

KENT: Oh.

BARBIE: Your name is almost like my old boyfriend's name.

KENT: That's exactly what I was going to say!

BARBIE: Really? Your girlfriend's name sounded like Barbie?

KENT: No.

BARBIE: *(Confused.)* Oh.

KENT: My old boyfriend's name is Barney.

BARBIE: *(Confused.)* Oh. I miss my old boyfriend.

KENT: Me, too.

(*BARBIE and KENT sigh. They try to eat lunch, but*

cannot reach their mouths. Suddenly, they realize they can feed each other. ALAN wakes up.)

ALAN: Um, excuse me. Um, sorry to interrupt, but . . . You see . . . I know that you have a lot of guys, um, trying to . . . who like you, but . . . I'm a nice guy. I know people say nice guys finish last, but . . . The thing is . . . I'll treat you right. Anytime you want a napkin, I'll be there. And—and—and I'll try my best not to, um, faint or anything. I mean, I won't once I get to know you. I'm actually a confident person. I'm a very informed person. Intelligent. So I've got that going for me, too. Like if you need help with your homework—not that you would! I'm not saying you're dumb or anything! I mean, I know just because a person has . . . because a person is beautiful doesn't mean that they aren't intelligent, but if you did need some help, I'm your guy. So . . . that's it. I'm Alan, by the way. And, well, you're—I'm—I think I'd be a really good boyfriend. I think.

BARBIE: *(To KENT.)* He's nice. I like him.

KENT: Me, too.

TALK BACK!

1. Can a person be genuinely positive all of the time? Do you like people who are positive or do you think they are phony? Why?

2. In Scene 1, which girl are you most like or would you most like to know? Why?

3. Would you judge Barbie based on her looks alone? Be honest. If your answer is yes, what about her looks would make you judge her, and would the judgment be positive or negative?

4. Do you think there's a difference between the kind of person you date and the kind of person you marry? Why or why not? If so, what are the differences between the two types?

5. Do you have a "type" you're attracted to? Do you find there's one trait you seek over and over again?

I WARNED YOU

3F, 3M

WHO

FEMALES	MALES
Gaby	Lance
Grace	Percy
Sunita	Wayne

WHERE Wayne and Grace's living room.

WHEN Saturday morning, present day.

In Scene 1, Grace and Wayne must create a convincing brother-sister relationship. The actors should be totally comfortable with each other and not afraid of looking silly or being annoying or cruel. In Scene 2, Wayne should be totally convincing until the moment his secret is revealed.

Write a scene that explores the brother-sister bond. The dialogue can be positive or negative. The goal is to make it sound as real and conversational as possible. (Hint: Sometimes it helps to eavesdrop and write down real conversations. Plus, it's fun.)

Scene 1: Wearing

GRACE: What are you doing?

WAYNE: Nothing.

GRACE: You must be doing something.

WAYNE: No.

GRACE: Wanna do something?

WAYNE: No.

GRACE: Why not?

WAYNE: Why would I do something with you?

GRACE: Why not?

WAYNE: What do you want, Grace?

GRACE: I want you to drive me to the mall.

WAYNE: What for?

GRACE: I want to look at stuff.

WAYNE: Stuff you can't buy.

GRACE: Why not?

WAYNE: Because it's not logical.

GRACE: Why does it need to be logical?

WAYNE: Because that's the way people are supposed to behave.

GRACE: Says who?

WAYNE: Says me. Says everyone. Now go away.

GRACE: Well, it is logical anyway. My birthday is coming up soon.

WAYNE: In a *month*.

GRACE: So? I should know what to ask for.

WAYNE: It doesn't require that much planning.

GRACE: Yes, it does.

WAYNE: No, it doesn't.

GRACE: How do you know?

WAYNE: I have birthdays, too.

GRACE: Yeah, but you're a guy.

WAYNE: So?

GRACE: So, for example, if you wanted a shirt, it would be no big deal. It would be a no-brainer. All guys' stuff looks the same.

WAYNE: No, it doesn't.

GRACE: Yes, it does. Your decisions are like short sleeves or long sleeves? Button front or tee?

Blue or green? It's nothing. It's minor. It's hard to go wrong. The only way a guy can get picked on for his clothes is if he wears something *really* bad or something that doesn't fit. And that's hard to do. On the other hand, girls have to be so specific. We have a lot more choices. And there's a lot more room for mistakes. A tiny misstep fashion-wise can make you a complete outsider at school. We have a lot more colors to choose from and styles and lengths and designs—

WAYNE: I don't care, OK? Can you just leave me alone?

GRACE: No.

WAYNE: Can't you shop online or something?

GRACE: Wayne, you're so dumb sometimes. I cannot shop online because one, I do not have a credit card and two, you don't actually know what things are going to look like on your body from a picture on a computer screen.

WAYNE: Sure you do.

GRACE: Plus, you don't know if the fabric feels slimy or if it's cheaply made—

WAYNE: That's why things have a price tag.

GRACE: You can't tell from the price if it's good quality or not! God, Wayne, you can be so dumb!

WAYNE: You're driving me crazy! Just shut up!

GRACE: **Just drive me to the mall.**

WAYNE: Ask someone else!

GRACE: There's no one else to ask! You're my brother. You have to.

WAYNE: No, I don't!

GRACE: Yes, you do!

WAYNE: No, I don't!

GRACE: Wayne, I'm not going to leave you alone.

WAYNE: **Shop online!**

GRACE: I can't!

WAYNE: You aren't going to buy anything anyway if you're just looking for your birthday so what difference does it make if you don't have a credit card? And you can check things out quality-wise another day. Just do it and leave me alone already. I'm not taking you to the mall.

GRACE: I'm not going to leave you alone, Wayne.

WAYNE: What is your problem? Why are you so annoying? Being annoying is not going to help you get your way. I am *less* likely to do what you want if you pester me, not *more*. I am determined at this point to never, ever drive you anywhere, especially the mall. I hope you never get to shop again. I hope you die a hundred years from now wearing the same clothes you have on now.

GRACE: Wayne, that is a horrible thing to say!

WAYNE: Why is that horrible? I said I wanted you to die a hundred years from now, not this minute. I think I was being nice. So just leave me alone. I want to have a quiet Sunday being a couch potato, especially since Mom and Dad are out of the house for once.

GRACE: You'll have a much quieter day if you drive me to the mall.

WAYNE: If I drive you to the mall, you'll want me to drive you back, too. And it's a twenty-minute drive each way. And I'll have to listen to you talk and play with the radio all the way there. No way.

GRACE: You can listen to me for twenty minutes on the way to the mall or for several hours if you don't.

WAYNE: There's no way going to the mall is that important. Just get over yourself and leave me alone. Life doesn't always go your way, Grace.

GRACE: Yes, it does.

WAYNE: Not today.

GRACE: I'll break you.

WAYNE: I'll break you in half if you don't shut up.

GRACE: You wouldn't. You'd go to prison.

WAYNE: Stop being immature.

GRACE: You're being immature. And selfish.

WAYNE: I'm selfish?

GRACE: You're only thinking of yourself. What *you* want to do today. Meanwhile, I'm trapped.

WAYNE: Oh, I feel really sorry for you.

GRACE: *You* have a car, I don't.

WAYNE: I earned that car. I paid for it myself. I worked every day practically bussing tables to pay for that car.

GRACE: I know.

WAYNE: So, I can do what I want with it. And I can finally relax a little. So that's what I'm going to do.

GRACE: No, you're not.

WAYNE: Yes, I am, Grace. End of story.

GRACE: This story is not over until I'm at the mall.

WAYNE: You're a loser, Grace.

GRACE: *I'm* a loser? Because I want to look good and have friends and do something out in society, I'm a loser? I don't think you know what a loser is.

WAYNE: I do. I looked it up in the dictionary and saw your picture.

GRACE: Wow. You're a funny guy, Wayne.

WAYNE: We have the same gene pool.

GRACE: Come on. Please?

WAYNE: Grace, leave me alone. You know if you didn't fail your drivers' test, you wouldn't have this problem.

GRACE: Thanks for rubbing it in. I can't parallel park, OK? Is that a crime?

WAYNE: It should be. As it stands, it just means you can't drive.

GRACE: When do people parallel park anyway? It doesn't come up that often.

WAYNE: I don't make the rules. Why don't you go to your room and write your congressman about it or something?

GRACE: You sound like Dad. That is really scary.

WAYNE: Whatever.

GRACE: You're turning into Dad. See what sitting on the couch does to a person? You're turning old right in front of my eyes.

WAYNE: Oh, horrors! I'm so scared!

GRACE: You should be.

WAYNE: I'm not.

GRACE: You should be.

WAYNE: You're driving me nuts!

GRACE: You're driving me to the mall!

WAYNE: No!

GRACE: Yes!

WAYNE: No!

GRACE: Yes!

WAYNE: No!

GRACE: Yes!

Scene 2: Worn

(WAYNE sits in a chair and stares straight ahead. SUNITA, GABY, PERCY, and LANCE enter.)

SUNITA: Oh my God, look at him!

PERCY: Wow. I thought it was a joke, but . . .

GABY: This is serious. Wayne? Hi! It's us. Sunita, Percy, Lance, and Gaby. Remember us? We go to the same school. We're your sister's friends.

(WAYNE continues staring straight ahead.)

LANCE: Wayne?

(LANCE waves his hand in front of WAYNE's face. Long beat where nothing happens. Slowly, WAYNE turns to face LANCE.)

LANCE: Hey! It's me! Lance! Grace's friend. How you doing?

(WAYNE turns to face forward again.)

PERCY: He is gone.

SUNITA: How could this be? He was fine yesterday.

(GRACE enters.)

GRACE: He's faking. Help me snap him out of it.

GABY: How can you say that?

GRACE: He just didn't want to take me to the mall.

SUNITA: No one would go mental just to get out of taking you to the mall.

PERCY: Wait. Did you expect him to go shopping with you, too?

GABY: Percy!

PERCY: What?

GABY: You're not funny.

PERCY: I'm not trying to be funny.

GRACE: *(To WAYNE.)* **Well, loser, you've really done it now! I hope you're proud of yourself! Now Mom and Dad will be so worried about you that *no one* will take me to the mall! I'm never going to get there again. And probably everyone will forget about my birthday so all my comparison shopping will go to waste. Thanks a lot, moron.**

GABY: Grace! How can you talk to him like that?

GRACE: He's faking!

LANCE: Wait. So what happened, anyway?

GRACE: **We were just having a conversation about him taking me to the mall since Mom and Dad were out, and he put his hands to his head and starting rocking back and forth, back and forth saying, "No. No. No. No." Over and over again. Just like that. "No. No. No. No. No." It got really** boring. And he did it for, like, an hour. If anyone should be mental here, it should be me. I had to listen to him say no for *ages*. So then I called you guys. He's been like this for about twenty minutes. At least he shut up.

WAYNE: No. No. No. No.

SUNITA: Grace, don't be heartless. There's obviously something wrong with him.

GRACE: Oh, there's something wrong with him. It's just not what you think is wrong with him.

PERCY: What's wrong with him, then?

GRACE: He's selfish.

GABY: Grace! Don't be horrible!

GRACE: He just wants attention. It's pathetic. *(In WAYNE's ear.)* You're pathetic, Wayne!

GABY: *(Pulling GRACE away from WAYNE.)* Stop it! Grace, what if you're wrong? What if he's really lost it?

GRACE: I would be very surprised.

LANCE: But what if it's true? What if you drove him over the edge?

GRACE: What do you mean what if *I* drove him over the edge?

LANCE: You were the last person to talk to him.

GRACE: He's faking.

PERCY: But what if he's not? Look. *(To WAYNE.)* Take me to the mall.

WAYNE: No! No. No. No. No.

SUNITA: It *is* your fault!

GRACE: No, it's not! All I did was ask him a question. What's so bad about that? Look, I called you guys over here to *help* me, not to blame me for Wayne's stupidity. Now which one of you is going to bring me to the mall?

PERCY: You're kidding, right?

GRACE: No. I want to go to the mall.

GABY: You've reduced your brother to a blithering idiot, and you want us to take you to the mall?

GRACE: Well, one of you has to have a car. You got here, didn't you?

LANCE: That's not the point.

GRACE: Well, it should be.

GABY: What's important here is that Wayne gets better.

SUNITA: I think I have an idea. But the rest of you have to go away for a couple of minutes.

LANCE: Why?

PERCY: Don't be an idiot. Come on.

(GABY, GRACE, PERCY, and LANCE exit.)

SUNITA: Hi, Wayne. It's Sunita. *(Beat.)* I came to see you when I heard you weren't feeling well. *(Beat.)* I want you to feel better, Wayne. Is there anything I can do? *(Beat.)* Help me out here, Wayne. *(Beat.)* Well, maybe I can think of something. You know you're very handsome, Wayne. I always thought so. I was just afraid to say it. You're a great guy. We've known each other for a long time. We get along really well, don't we? I think so. I think we do. *(Beat.)* But I've always wondered, Wayne, how come . . . I'm friends with your sister, but I've always thought we sort of had something together. *(Beat.)* You've very easy to talk to. You have a great sense of humor. I like you. So . . . *(Beat. SUNITA leans in and kisses WAYNE on the cheek.)* Did you like that, Wayne? Give me some sign. I've always thought you liked me, too. Like that time we were watching that scary movie and we were sitting together on the couch? When I was scared you put your arm around me, remember? That was really nice. Wayne? Can you hear me?

WAYNE: I think . . . Maybe if you kiss me again—

SUNITA: I knew I could cure you!

(WAYNE starts laughing.)

WAYNE: Shhh! She'll hear you.

SUNITA: What? Wayne! *(Standing.)* You were faking! And I—I can't believe you! I hate you!

WAYNE: Shhh!

SUNITA: How could you do that to me?

WAYNE: Shhh! Come here.

SUNITA: No!

WAYNE: Come on.

SUNITA: No way! You betrayed me.

WAYNE: I what?

SUNITA: You deceived me.

WAYNE: It wasn't on purpose.

SUNITA: I was worried! I thought you were dying or something or I never would have said those things.

WAYNE: It's OK.

SUNITA: It's not OK.

WAYNE: But I didn't mind it.

SUNITA: Of course you didn't mind it. I hate you.

WAYNE: What? I was just trying to teach Grace a lesson.

SUNITA: Well, that's a terrible way to do it. We all thought you were actually injured or something.

WAYNE: I was sick of listening to her.

SUNITA: So you cooked this up?

WAYNE: Shhh! Come sit next to me.

SUNITA: No way! *(Yelling.)* You guys? Come in here!

WAYNE: Don't say anything, Sunita. Don't. Please.

(PERCY, GABY, LANCE, and GRACE enter. WAYNE goes back to acting catatonic.)

SUNITA: I think we should call the mental hospital. He's not faking. He's snapped.

GABY: Maybe we should.

PERCY: We can't commit him. We're not his family or anything. We should just wait until his family comes home.

GRACE: I'm his family. Let's put him away.

GABY: Grace!

SUNITA: No, she's right.

LANCE: You guys, this is serious. I've seen movies about this. Once you get in, it's almost impossible to get out. And they might give him a lobotomy.

GRACE: What's the difference? He's already brainless.

GABY: Grace, stop. Let's be serious here.

SUNITA: Lance, you've only seen one movie, haven't you?

LANCE: Well, yeah, but it was very vivid.

PERCY: And untrue. That's not what it's like. He'll just see psychiatrists.

SUNITA: And they might tie him to a bed and give him electroshock therapy sometimes.

PERCY: No.

SUNITA: It could happen.

GRACE: Who knows? It might improve his personality.

GABY: Sunita, what happened in here while we were gone?

SUNITA: Nothing. I tried to talk to him.

GABY: I would have thought you'd be the last person to suggest we put him in a hospital. You have a crush on—

SUNITA: No, I don't!

GABY: Sure you do! You have for years.

SUNITA: No, I haven't. I've met someone else.

GABY: Who?

SUNITA: Someone who's not mental. Or cruel.

GABY: Cruel.

SUNITA: Hey! I've got an idea. Let's poke him with sticks to see if he'll respond.

LANCE: There are lots of forks in the kitchen.

WAYNE: No. No. No. No.

GRACE: Let's do it. He needs help. We need to snap him out of it.

PERCY: It's worth a try.

WAYNE: No! No! No! No!

SUNITA: Poor guy.

LANCE: Let's get some utensils.

GABY: You guys, this is crazy!

(LANCE, GRACE, PERCY, and GABY exit.)

WAYNE: Sunita, don't do this! I'm sorry.

SUNITA: Then you'd better call me.

(LANCE, GRACE, PERCY, and GABY enter.)

PERCY: We got you a bucket of cold water to pour on his head, Sunita.

SUNITA: Perfect.

GRACE: You could have just taken me to the mall, Wayne. You chose this.

TALK BACK!

1. No matter how old you get, you always fall into the same patterns with your family. Do you think this statement is true? What role do you play in your family?

2. What are some techniques you use to manipulate people into doing what you want? What do you think Grace could have done differently to get Wayne to drive her to the mall?

3. Have you ever had a joke backfire on you, like Wayne does? What happened? Do you like practical jokes? Why or why not?

4. Why do you think females are usually more interested in shopping than males? Is this a genetic thing or something instilled by the media? What do you think are general personality traits that separate males from females?

5. What might you do to get Wayne to "snap out of it"?

6. Who is the cruelest character: Wayne, Grace, or Sunita? Why?

SWORN ENEMY

4F, 2M

WHO

FEMALES   MALES
Charlotte   Hudson
Joanne   Jared
Lyddie
Narnia

WHERE Scene 1: A classroom; Scene 2: The school parking lot.

WHEN Present day.

🎭 Think about what makes a group cool and uncool. See if you can *subtly* reflect these traits in your characters while still making them seem real. What similar traits bind these friends together?

✍ Scene: Bully vs. geek. Explore the comic possibilities and see if you can come up with a few surprises.

Scene 1: Incident in Room 3B

LYDDIE: Want to do karaoke tonight?

JARED: Sure!

NARNIA: We could go to the pancake house beforehand.

LYDDIE: So, after school?

JARED: Sounds good.

> (CHARLOTTE *walks in with JOANNE and HUDSON.*)

LYDDIE: Oh no.

NARNIA: You can't come?

LYDDIE: No, no! It's not that. It's *her.*

JARED: Who?

LYDDIE: *Her.*

JARED: Oh.

NARNIA: It's OK. We're here.

LYDDIE: She's horrible. I hate her so much. Let's stand in the hall.

NARNIA: You can't let her run your life.

LYDDIE: What is she doing in here? This isn't her room.

JARED: Yeah, but she's friends with Hudson and Joanne.

NARNIA: Remember when Hudson was this skinny little geek with braces? Now he's like the school hunk. Weird, huh?

LYDDIE: How come that couldn't happen for us?

JARED: Speak for yourself!

NARNIA: Maybe it still will.

LYDDIE: Yeah, right.

NARNIA: It's not impossible.

LYDDIE: Those people rule the school. And they hate me. Charlotte Pullman has been picking on me since second grade. Barring extensive plastic surgery and a personality makeover, nothing's going to change that now. Just look at her.

(CHARLOTTE, HUDSON, and JOANNE mime talking to each other.)

LYDDIE: I bet she's plotting how to make my life complete hell. She's probably saying, "Look at Lyddie's shirt. It looks used and dirty and old." People shop at thrift stores! I can't help that I don't have the money to shop at expensive places. She is such a bitch! Once she made up this song, "Lyddie, Lyddie, not so pretty, has a mouth like Hello Kitty." Sure it sounds stupid now, Hello Kitty doesn't even have a mouth, but it really hurt my feelings at the time. And she got a whole bunch of people to sing it with her whenever they saw me. She's evil. I can't wait 'til I go off to college and I never see her again. Until I become famous, and I become her boss.

JARED: She gets really good grades. She'll probably get into a better college than you. Maybe she'll be *your* boss.

LYDDIE: Thanks a lot, Jared. You're a really great boyfriend.

NARNIA: Dare to dream, girl. You could be her boss. I'm sure of it.

LYDDIE: Thanks, Narnia.

NARNIA: Once she gets out of here, who knows what will happen to her? She won't be the big fish in the little pond anymore. She'll be a nobody, just like us.

JARED: I'm not a nobody. I'm the first chair oboe in the orchestra. Suck on that, Hudson Hunk!

LYDDIE: I wish I had your self-esteem, Jared.

JARED: Why don't you?

LYDDIE: It doesn't work like that. You can't just decide that you're going to have self-esteem.

JARED: Why not?

NARNIA: Boys are so simple.

LYDDIE: I know. It must be so nice.

JARED: Girls just make things too complicated. You just need to have fun. You don't even like what those girls like. Would you really want to sit around painting your toenails and talking on your cell phone all day?

LYDDIE: Well . . .

NARNIA: Not *exactly* . . .

JARED: Please. You're both musical, and I think you're cool. We have fun, right? When we go out and do karaoke?

NARNIA: Definitely. But don't you ever wish even a little bit for more, Jared? You know? Just to have a little bit more money or friends or popularity?

JARED: Naw. I don't want more. I wouldn't complain if I got more money or friends or popularity, but I'm not going to be someone else to get it. Why should I? I'm me and I'm terrific. Or at least that's what my mom tells me. And I'm not going to call my mom a liar! She's a smart woman.

LYDDIE: She is. You're the best.

JARED: I *am* the best! The best boyfriend, the best oboe player—what more could a guy ask for? Except, I guess, to have friends who are happy, too. So stop worrying about Charlotte Pullman. Know what I think of her? I think she wears too much makeup and she talks too much and she's too tan. She's trying too hard. I like people who are natural and real. If you're fake, you're not my kind of person.

NARNIA: You're so deep and cool, Jared.

JARED: I know.

NARNIA: We should feel good about ourselves. All of us. We're awesome.

LYDDIE: We are. I guess.

NARNIA: We are!

LYDDIE: Right. *(Beat.)* I still wish I were Charlotte Pullman.

JARED: You're impossible!

LYDDIE: But you guys still love me!

NARNIA: I guess we're crazy, too.

(CHARLOTTE gets up and crosses past LYDDIE, JARED, and NARNIA to leave. CHARLOTTE throws her bag over her shoulder, hitting LYDDIE. Unaware of what she's done, CHARLOTTE continues walking and exits.)

LYDDIE: Did you see that? Thanks a lot! What an evil wench! Why is she so mean to me?

JOANNE: *(To LYDDIE)* Hey, come over here.

LYDDIE: *(To NARNIA and JARED.)* Is she joking? No way! She wants to torture me. As if!

JOANNE: You! Girl with the sweater! Come over here for a sec. We want to tell you something.

LYDDIE: No, thanks.

HUDSON: We just want to tell you something.

LYDDIE: I'm busy.

(HUDSON and JOANNE exchange a look.)

LYDDIE: I knew they were talking about me. They're relentless. What did I ever do to them?

NARNIA: Nothing. Just ignore them.

JOANNE: What's her problem?

HUDSON: Beats me.

LYDDIE: I can't take this anymore! It's relentless!

JARED: Calm down. It's all gonna be OK.

LYDDIE: No! I have to get this torment to stop! I'm going to challenge Charlotte to a duel.

NARNIA: People don't duel anymore.

JARED: With what? Swords? Guns?

LYDDIE: I don't know. Wits. Fists.

NARNIA: You're going to fight her?

LYDDIE: I have to show her that she and her friends can't pick on me anymore. I have to stand up for myself. For practically my whole life, I've been enduring humiliation. I'm done. I'm through with it.

I don't want to live in fear anymore. I am going to stand up for what's good and right for my sake and for the sake of every unpopular girl in school.

NARNIE: Lyddie!

JARED: Are you sure this is a good idea?

LYDDIE: Yes! I mean, I don't want to, but I have to!

(CHARLOTTE reenters.)

JARED: Here's your chance.

NARNIA: Are you sure, Lyddie?

LYDDIE: No!

JARED: But you said you would.

LYDDIE: But it's wrong to fight, right?

NARNIA: Not if it's a bully.

LYDDIE: Well . . . OK. Here I go.

(LYDDIE stands still.)

JARED: You're moving very slowly.

LYDDIE: Shut up! I'm going to do this.

(Beat.)

NARNIA: You don't have to if you don't want to.

LYDDIE: No. I want to.

(LYDDIE walks up to CHARLOTTE.)

LYDDIE: I'm sick of you tormenting me. I challenge you to a fight! If I win, you leave me alone forever. If you win, I get beat up and look pathetic, obviously. So, what's it going to be, Charlotte?

CHARLOTTE: What?

LYDDIE: After school in the parking lot. Be there or be . . .

(LYDDIE draws a square shape in the air with her fingers.)

NARNIA: Lyddie, are you crazy?

LYDDIE: Come on, let's go before I lose my nerve.

(LYDDIE, NARNIA, and JARED exit.)

CHARLOTTE: Who *is* that girl?

Scene 2: Day of Reckoning

LYDDIE: Oh my God, did I really say, "Be there or be square"? I am an idiot!

JARED: No, you told her, "Be there or be . . ."

(JARED draws a square shape in the air with his fingers.)

LYDDIE: I'm such a dork!

NARNIA: You don't have to do this. I didn't imagine when you went over to talk to her that you'd actually challenge her to a fight! I thought maybe you'd go over there and tell her to leave you alone and get ostracized for life, maybe, but fighting? No. It doesn't make sense, Lyddie. You're not the fighting kind. And it's wrong anyway. It doesn't solve anything. Look at war. Does it actually stop other wars from happening? Do people learn from the experience? No. People who like to fight just keep fighting. War doesn't bring peace and this fight with Charlotte is a suicide mission. You'll never win any way you look at it.

LYDDIE: Thanks a lot. I feel great now.

NARNIA: I'm sorry to say it, but it's true.

LYDDIE: I'm trying to get respect here, Narnia. I'm trying to get her to leave me alone once and for all. Desperate times call for desperate measures.

NARNIA: I've been thinking about it. I don't think

you'll gain her respect. Or popularity. Or that she'll back off. It could have the opposite effect. That's just something you see on TV. It could get worse.

JARED: I don't know. I think it might work. I've seen things like that work a bunch of times. That's how guys settle things. We fight about something and it's done. Like look at me, for example. I'm in the band. I get pretty good grades. My idea of a good time is singing karaoke or writing science-fiction stories. I never, ever watch football. I could be dead right now, seriously, if I didn't learn to fight every once in a while. Fortunately, I'm pretty quick and I've got a good right punch. Usually if you show a guy you can face him in a fight, he'll leave you alone and find an easier target.

NARNIA: But girls are different. We're vindictive and catty. I hate to say it, I do, but we don't let things go that easily. Charlotte might have a personal vendetta against you, Lyddie, for the rest of time. She could ruin your whole life.

JARED: That's a little melodramatic, don't you think? Lyddie can move away after high school, start a new life, and never see or think about Charlotte again.

NARNIA: Or not.

LYDDIE: You're not helping! Stop it, both of you! Shut up. You're making me more nervous. I'm already about to have a nervous breakdown. It is taking every bit of my willpower just to keep from running away from here screaming. But I think this is something I have to do. It can't get worse. It can't!

Charlotte has been after me from day one of my life, practically. I can't take it anymore. I won't take it anymore. I have to be free of this tyranny! Today is the day. Whatever happens, happens. I have to face up to this. That's her car over there, right? She has to come back here soon.

JARED: Unless she's chickened out.

NARNIA: Or actually taken the high road.

LYDDIE: Whose side are you on, Narnia?

NARNIA: Yours, of course. I just think this isn't a good idea.

JARED: It's definitely her car. The license plate says, "CHAR GR8."

LYDDIE: That's so stupid. I hate her even more now.

NARNIA: Here she comes with Hudson and Joanne!

LYDDIE: Oh my God! I'm freaking out!

(*CHARLOTTE, HUDSON, and JOANNE enter and walk across the stage. When they are almost off-stage, LYDDIE jumps in front of CHARLOTTE.*)

LYDDIE: Wh-where are you going?

CHARLOTTE: To my car, of course.

LYDDIE: Are you going to run, then?

CHARLOTTE: I'm going to drive. That's why I'm going to my car.

LYDDIE: Well, what about us?

CHARLOTTE: Us?

LYDDIE: The, uh, fight. Today.

CHARLOTTE: Oh, right. Um, are you sure you've got the right person?

LYDDIE: Charlotte Pullman.

CHARLOTTE: Right, that's me. I mean, if you want to fight, we can fight, but, frankly, I don't know who you are.

LYDDIE: Excuse me?

CHARLOTTE: Who the hell are you?

LYDDIE: Lyddie? Lyddie Grubner?

CHARLOTTE: Lyddie Grubner, I don't know you. We're not friends. What's the problem here?

LYDDIE: You've been tormenting me my whole life!

CHARLOTTE: You must have me confused with some-one else.

LYDDIE: Give me a break! Even earlier today you were getting your cronies here to pick on me.

JOANNE: What?

HUDSON: She's talking about in homeroom.

JOANNE: Oh, right. Your tag was sticking out of your shirt. I was going to tell you and you went all psycho on me.

HUDSON: Maybe you need some medication.

JARED: Hey, that's my girlfriend.

HUDSON: So?

JARED: So, I'm saying that's not very nice.

HUDSON: I just call it like I see it.

CHARLOTTE: Anyway, we have to go now. We have things to do.

LYDDIE: So you're running away?

CHARLOTTE: *I don't know you.* I've got no problem with you Linda—

LYDDIE: Lyddie—

CHARLOTTE: —except that you're getting in my way.

LYDDIE: But you pushed me and you made up a song about Hello Kitty and you called me names and talked about my clothes . . .

CHARLOTTE: No offense, but you have an inflated sense of your own importance.

LYDDIE: Excuse me?

CHARLOTTE: I don't remember any of that stuff. And for me to be "tormenting" you, as you say, would mean that I've have to sit around plotting and planning. I don't do that. I don't have time. I have other things to think about. And I'm not a bully. Ask anyone.

LYDDIE: I don't need to ask anyone. I've experienced your bullying first hand.

CHARLOTTE: Well, you're wrong.

LYDDIE: No, I'm not.

CHARLOTTE: Get out of my way, geek.

LYDDIE: See?

CHARLOTTE: You're forcing me to ridicule you. This is the most ridiculous thing I've ever seen.

HUDSON: Listen, this is fun, but we have somewhere to go.

JARED: Back off. This is none of your business.

HUDSON: Look, we're minding our own business. It's you weirdos that are holding things up here.

JOANNE: I don't know if you've heard, but school is over and I for one would like to get out of here.

NARNIA: Don't be condescending.

JOANNE: Why not?

NARNIA: Because it's rude.

JOANNE: *(Mocking.)* "Because it's rude!"

(NARNIA throws a punch at JOANNE. JOANNE ducks and NARNIA hits JARED. JARED throws up his arm to gain his balance and hits LYDDIE in the head, knocking her out.)

NARNIA: Oh my God!

JARED: Are you OK?

(NARNIA and JARED rush over to LYDDIE. HUDSON, JOANNE, and CHARLOTTE step over LYDDIE.)

HUDSON: Is she in our grade?

JOANNE: I think she's younger. She acts younger.

CHARLOTTE: What's her name again? Lindy?

HUDSON: No clue.

(HUDSON, JOANNE, and CHARLOTTE exit. LYDDIE wakes up.)

LYDDIE: What happened? Is it over?

NARNIA: Um, yeah.

LYDDIE: Did I show her how it is?

JARED: Well, she knows where you stand.

LYDDIE: Where is she?

JARED: She had to leave.

LYDDIE: I hope she's not too injured. I just wanted to hurt her a little.

NARNIA: Well, she did seem a little upset that you called her a bully.

LYDDIE: Free at last!

TALK BACK!

1. Have you ever had to deal with a bully? How did you handle it?

2. Do boys fight differently than girls? If so, how?

3. What's the best way to get someone to stop picking on you?

4. Have you ever picked on someone? If so, why? What makes a person stand out as a victim?

5. If a person wanted to change their social standing, how should he or she go about it? Is it possible?

6. Do you think Jared's self-esteem is real? Do you admire him for it or think he's a dork?

7. Do you think Charlotte truly doesn't remember Lyddie or is she faking it?

ANYTHING YOU CAN DO

3F, 5M

WHO

FEMALES
Anne
Lola
Sunny

MALES
John
Michael
Michel
Pierce
Walker

WHERE Outside school.

WHEN Present day.

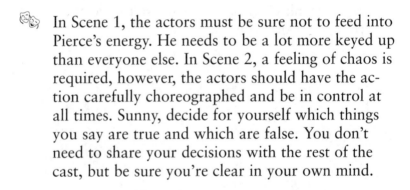

In Scene 1, the actors must be sure not to feed into Pierce's energy. He needs to be a lot more keyed up than everyone else. In Scene 2, a feeling of chaos is required, however, the actors should have the action carefully choreographed and be in control at all times. Sunny, decide for yourself which things you say are true and which are false. You don't need to share your decisions with the rest of the cast, but be sure you're clear in your own mind.

Think of a crazy lie, like you're dating a Playboy model. Now write a play where it's come true, and see how your family and friends react to your amazing new life.

Je me suis ennuyé sans toi = I was bored without you.
Je me suis ennuyé sans toi, aussi = I was bored without you, too.

164

Scene 1: No, You Can't

WALKER: Yeah. We went to Europe this summer.

LOLA: That's cool.

WALKER: It would be cooler if my parents didn't come, too.

ANNE: Yeah, but they paid for it, right?

WALKER: How could I forget? They reminded me of that every day.

JOHN: But you got to meet foreign chicks, right?

WALKER: Well, yeah. As much as you can when you're with your parents and no one speaks the same language. Of course we didn't go to any Spanish-speaking countries. That would be too easy. I'd have a fighting chance of getting by since I take Spanish. But no. We went to France and Italy and Germany. None of us speak those languages, not even my parents. How smart is that? And my dad is the kind of guy who thinks if he talks loud enough and waves his hands around people will understand him. We were the American tourist stereotype. It was so embarrassing. Why are parents twice as embarrassing when they're wearing Bermuda shorts? Winter clothes are bad enough, but somehow summer clothes are infinitely worse. There's more skin, I guess. And the last thing you want to see is your mother's leg skin. Plus, people in Europe don't really wear shorts. We looked like idiots. Cameras around our necks, bad sunglasses—the whole nine. My mom even tried to get me to wear a fanny pack.

PIERCE: Did you?

WALKER: No way! **I'd rather be robbed and killed and thrown in a ditch than wear a fanny pack.**

JOHN: So did you get any foreign chick action?

WALKER: My parents wouldn't let me alone for a single minute. **It was a nightmare.**

SUNNY: I went to Europe. I went everywhere.

WALKER: Did you go to Paris?

SUNNY: Of course. I went everywhere.

LOLA: You can't really have gone everywhere.

SUNNY: We did.

PIERCE: That's not actually possible.

SUNNY: I managed to learn every language, too. I wanted to be able to communicate with the native people and not seem like a tourist.

PIERCE: OK, speak some Portuguese.

SUNNY: It's a lot like Spanish. I don't remember it now. I learned it on the train ride there.

WALKER: We saw the *Mona Lisa*—

SUNNY: I saw the *Mona Lisa*.

WALKER: —and it was so small.

SUNNY: Of course it's small.

WALKER: Didn't you think that was weird?

SUNNY: No. That's what I expected.

WALKER: I didn't.

ANNE: So where else did you go?

WALKER: Rome, Berlin—

SUNNY: I sang in a nightclub in Berlin.

PIERCE: What?

SUNNY: I sang in a nightclub in Berlin.

LOLA: Why?

SUNNY: They asked me to.

LOLA: Who asked you to?

PIERCE: She's lying.

SUNNY: Some guy. I guess he owned the club.
He heard me singing outside and asked me to do a
song onstage.

LOLA: So what did you sing?

PIERCE: She didn't.

SUNNY: I sang "At Last"—that old song they play at weddings? At least they did at my sister's wedding. And it was a jazz club, so I thought that would fit. And it did. It went over really well. I got a standing ovation. I sang it better than Christina Aguilera.

PIERCE: Right.

SUNNY: They asked me to sing again the next night, but I couldn't. I was busy.

PIERCE: Let me guess. The president wanted to have you over for dinner.

SUNNY: No, silly.

PIERCE: A film director begged you to be in his film.

SUNNY: No, but a photographer did ask to take my picture in Italy. The guys there wouldn't leave me alone. My butt hurt for weeks from all the pinching.

ANNE: They pinched you?

SUNNY: Yeah. All the time.

ANNE: And you let them?

SUNNY: I didn't have a choice.

JOHN: You're just that irresistible to Italians.

SUNNY: I guess so.

PIERCE: So speak some Dutch.

SUNNY: I told you that I learned it just for the trip.

PIERCE: Not even one word?

SUNNY: You need to learn to listen, Pierce.

PIERCE: You are such a liar.

LOLA: Pierce, you don't know that. She might be telling the truth.

PIERCE: **She sang in a nightclub in Germany? And got a standing ovation? I've seen her in school musicals. She's not that good.**

SUNNY: Shows what you know. I'm going to be an actress and singer. Dozens of people have told me I have what it takes.

ANNE: Some of the things you say, Sunny, are kind of unlikely.

PIERCE: **Unlikely? That's putting it mildly. How about impossible? You went *everywhere* in Europe? You learned *all* the languages they speak there? Unless there's some kind of mental disease going around Italy, there's no way *all* Italian men everywhere you went wanted to pinch your old butt. No way! You're lying. You lie constantly.**

SUNNY: You need some help. I know a lot about psychiatry, so I should know. You should get some psychotherapy or something.

PIERCE: That's another thing. You know everything. Everything! If anyone says anything, you answer, "I know." You know! You never say things first, you always chime in afterwards, "I knew that." Like the *Mona Lisa* thing. Walker said it was small and you said, "Of course. I knew that." So smug. Well, why don't you tell us about something else you saw in Europe?

SUNNY: The Eiffel Tower.

PIERCE: Tell us something about it we don't know.

SUNNY: When it's windy, it moves.

PIERCE: Oh. It moves. The Eiffel Tower moves if it gets windy. If that were true, it would be halfway across Europe by now.

WALKER: Um, that's kind of true. It's not that it *moves* exactly, it sways.

SUNNY: Exactly!

PIERCE: But you just agreed with him again.

LOLA: Well, she did say it first, Pierce.

PIERCE: But everyone knows about the Eiffel Tower. That's why you picked that.

SUNNY: I thought you wanted me to say something Walker could prove or disprove. Not that I need to prove myself to you. This is silly. You're just jealous.

PIERCE: I'm jealous? Jealous of what? The fact

that you lie all the time? I'm sorry to burst your bubble, but I'm not jealous of that. I'd rather be honest. I sat at home all summer because I broke my leg.

SUNNY: I broke both of my arms when I was little. I had to be fed.

PIERCE: See? See? Everything someone else says you have to top. You can't not be the center of attention.

SUNNY: You shouldn't use a double negative like that.

PIERCE: What?

SUNNY: Your grammar. It's bad.

PIERCE: It's poor.

SUNNY: No, it's bad.

PIERCE: It doesn't matter! The point is, how come you always have to top everyone? Maybe we wanted to hear about what Walker did this summer. Maybe we wanted to know more about his trip to Europe before you butted in and started telling dumb stories about things that never happened.

SUNNY: Fine with me. Go on, Walker.

WALKER: That was pretty much it. My parents wouldn't leave me alone so it wasn't that much fun.

(Beat.)

PIERCE: Well, OK. That's what I wanted to hear. Anyone else besides Sunny?

ANNE: You're being a little harsh.

PIERCE: Doesn't anyone else see how she lies? How she manipulates every conversation so it revolves around her?

LOLA: I think you're being harsh, too.

JOHN: Well, I'm not sure if I buy all of it, but we can't be sure, can we?

PIERCE: That's just it! She picks things that we can't refute! Like breaking both arms when she was little. None of us knew her then, so she could make it up!

JOHN: Did someone have to help you pee?

SUNNY: Yes.

JOHN: And . . . the rest of it?

SUNNY: Yep.

LOLA: No one would make that up. That's gross.

PIERCE: But it doesn't matter if it's good or bad, as long as she gets attention. I mean, why couldn't she just let Walker finish his story?

WALKER: It's OK. I was done.

PIERCE: It's not OK. Am I the only one who sees this?

SUNNY: Sorry if I upset you, Pierce. I was just making conversation.

PIERCE: Right. I can't believe you guys don't get this.

(PIERCE exits. Beat.)

JOHN: My dad and I went to a bunch of professional wrestling shows this summer. It was awesome.

SUNNY: I jello wrestled once. It was for charity. We made a lot of money. I won the match. I could be a professional wrestler.

Scene 2: Yes, I Can

SUNNY: I'm volunteering at the hospital.

ANNE: That's great.

LOLA: Yeah. I should do something to give back to the community, too.

SUNNY: They let me watch an appendectomy yesterday.

ANNE: They did?

SUNNY: Yeah.

LOLA: I would have fainted. I don't need to see my insides or anyone else's, thank you!

SUNNY: Well, I almost fainted, but this cute med student put his arm around me and told me everything would be OK.

ANNE: No way! How come med students never notice me?

LOLA: Yeah, but he was way too old, right?

SUNNY: When I was in France, I had a French boyfriend who was twenty-two.

LOLA: No way!

SUNNY: His name was Michel. He was rich, too.

ANNE: And your parents didn't mind?

SUNNY: No! They were cool. I stayed with him for three weeks.

LOLA: Oh my God! Then what?

SUNNY: Then we had to move on. I was so sad. We both were, Michel and me. He even cried. He told me he'd love me forever. I wanted to stay in France, but I couldn't.

LOLA: That is so romantic. Only in France! How come there are no romantic, sensitive guys like that here? Only I'd like one a little younger.

ANNE: But the older ones are more mature. I'd love to have a mature boyfriend.

LOLA: And French!

ANNE: Definitely!

SUNNY: And he was really hot. He was an artist and a model.

ANNE: Are you serious?

SUNNY: Yeah. His art was really beautiful.

ANNE: How come he never visited you?

SUNNY: We decided on having a clean break. It was better that way. He said I should meet a nice, American boy my own age.

LOLA: How romantic!

(MICHAEL enters and watches LOLA, SUNNY, and ANNE from a distance.)

ANNE: You are so lucky, Sunny. Everything good happens to you.

LOLA: Yeah, Sunny. You're like the luckiest person in the entire world!

MICHAEL: Sunny?

SUNNY: What?

MICHAEL: Sunny! It's me! Michael! From Paris!

(MICHAEL rushes over to SUNNY to give her a kiss on each cheek. Behind his back, LOLA and ANNE gasp and cover their noses and mouths in horror—MICHAEL smells.)

MICHAEL: Oh, Sunny! I thought I'd never see you again! Then I heard about this student exchange and I thought I'd try my luck.

SUNNY: Oh. Great.

ANNE: Oh wow. You are French.

MICHAEL: I'm not French. I'm from Indiana.

LOLA: But you met in France.

MICHAEL: Right.

ANNE: So why . . .

MICHAEL: What?

ANNE: Never mind.

LOLA: You look young.

MICHAEL: Thanks, I guess.

LOLA: Are you a lawyer?

SUNNY: This is Michael. Not Michel.

MICHAEL: What? Who's Michel?

ANNE: She had a boyfriend named Michel in Paris who was—

MICHAEL: I was her boyfriend in Paris.

SUNNY: No, no. You just *thought* you were my boyfriend.

MICHAEL: What? You cried when I had to leave to come back to Indiana.

LOLA: *She* cried?

MICHAEL: Yeah. And you said you'd love me forever—Then you hooked up with some other guy named Michel? Sunny, how could you? We were in love. We went to the Eiffel Tower together! That's what people do when they're in love.

SUNNY: That's what tourists do.

MICHAEL: I bought you flowers. We ate crepes!

Paris is the most romantic city in the world. And we traveled it together, hand-in-hand.

SUNNY: I don't recall any handholding.

MICHAEL: Why are you breaking my heart like this?

SUNNY: Um, yeah, I don't remember it how you remember it. Sorry about that.

MICHAEL: But you said you loved me. We're soul mates.

SUNNY: Well, no. I guess not.

MICHAEL: What?

SUNNY: You're my parents' high school friends' son.

MICHAEL: We've been practically promised to each other since birth, and in Paris . . . we had something. Don't deny it, Sunny. I don't know what's going on here. Maybe you—do you want to keep us a secret? So it will be just our thing? That's romantic. That's it, right? See how well I know you? You're so clever. Don't worry. I'll keep our secret, darling!

ANNE: So you're not French? But . . .

MICHAEL: What?

ANNE: Never mind.

LOLA: Maybe we should leave you two alone.

SUNNY: No, that's OK.

MICHAEL: That would be great.

(ANNE and LOLA cross to the other side of the stage.)

LOLA: Something's weird about this.

ANNE: I could hardly breathe!

LOLA: Do you think Sunny really went out with *him*?

ANNE: I don't know. Sounds like it. But right now, I just need some air!

(LOLA and ANNE exit.)

MICHAEL: Sunny, who is this Michael?

SUNNY: Michel. Well, he's an artist and a model.

MICHAEL: And you went out with him?

SUNNY: I did.

MICHAEL: You said you'd love me forever. Why did you cheat on me, on our love?

SUNNY: Well, I don't know about that.

(WALKER runs in.)

WALKER: Someone help!

MICHAEL: What?

(PIERCE stumbles in followed by LOLA, ANNE, and JOHN.)

PIERCE: I think my appendix is bursting! Someone, please help!

ANNE: Sunny! You saw that surgery yesterday! What do you remember?

(PIERCE collapses to the ground, moaning.)

LOLA: Do something! Hurry!

(MICHEL enters.)

MICHEL: Where is Sunny?

SUNNY: Michel!

MICHAEL: Michel? You bastard!

(MICHAEL lunges at MICHEL.)

SUNNY: No!

ANNE: He's for real? I'm so confused!

PIERCE: Help!

SUNNY: Does anyone have a Swiss army knife?

JOHN: I've got one in my locker.

SUNNY: Go get it.

(JOHN exits.)

MICHAEL: She's mine!

MICHEL: Who are you?

MICHAEL: I'm her boyfriend!

MICHEL: It can't be! I know I told you to find a nice, American boy, but this one stinks!

SUNNY: He's not my boyfriend, Michel!

(MICHAEL gets MICHEL into a headlock. SUNNY jumps on MICHAEL's back and quickly wrestles him to the ground.)

MICHAEL: Let me go!

SUNNY: If I let you go, will you leave me alone?

MICHAEL: You loved me!

SUNNY: No, I didn't!

MICHAEL: But—

(SUNNY twists his arm behind his back.)

MICHAEL: Ow! Ow! OK! OK!

(SUNNY lets MICHAEL go. MICHAEL exits.)

MICHEL: My darling! You are amazing!

SUNNY: Oh, Michel! You're here!

MICHEL: I have a modeling job here and I just had

to see you. I have missed you so much. You are my sun, my moon, my stars—

(JOHN enters with a Swiss army knife.)

JOHN: Here!

WALKER: What are you going to do?

SUNNY: I'm going to operate. I saw this surgery yester-day in the hospital. I can do it.

WALKER: Are you sure?

(SUNNY kneels down next to PIERCE.)

JOHN: This is cool!

(SUNNY opens the knife and pulls up PIERCE's shirt.)

PIERCE: Wait!

SUNNY: What? Hold still!

PIERCE: No! Stop!

SUNNY: But I'm going to save your life!

PIERCE: No!

(PIERCE stands.)

PIERCE: I'm fine!

SUNNY: Don't be scared. I can do this.

PIERCE: No, I'm really fine. And I'll never doubt you again.

SUNNY: What?

MICHEL: Darling, he's fine. You take my breath away with your quick thinking! You are just as I remember you. Although you are more beautiful than ever. And I remember you being pretty beautiful. So that is to say that you are very, very beautiful, indeed. And I should know, because I am French and we love beautiful things. I know we have been so far away these last few months, but you are always close to my heart, my little Sunny. You are always *(Points to his heart.)* here. And I know I am too old and too French for you. You deserve a nice, clean, American boy. But while I am here, while I am near to you . . . Can we not pretend, if only for a moment, that our love can last? We must seize the moment! Let's go be alone somewhere together. *Je me suis ennuyé sans vous.*

SUNNY: *Je me suis ennuyé sans vous, aussi.*

(MICHEL and SUNNY exit.)

PIERCE: I can't believe it. Climbing Everest, starring in that Scorsese film—it must all be true.

JOHN: Unbelievable.

PIERCE: Completely unbelievable.

TALK BACK!

1. Have you ever told a big lie that wasn't to spare someone's feelings or to cover up a wrongdoing (in other words, just for the fun of it)? To whom did you tell it and why?

2. Why do you think some people compulsively lie? What do they get out of it?

3. Do you think you'd find Sunny annoying or amusing?

4. Do you think all of Sunny's stories are true? Do you think all of Sunny's stories are lies? Why?

5. If you could tell a lie about yourself and have everyone believe it, what would it be and why?

6. How can you make a lie seem convincing? Are there any telltale signs that give away a liar?

THE LESSON

3F

WHO
FEMALES
Emmy
Reagan
Vanessa

WHERE Scene 1: A school hallway; Scene 2: A basement recording studio.

WHEN Present day.

Vanessa and Emmy: You can be as dramatic as you'd like as long as you believe what you say. If you commit to your character then nothing is over the top.

Write a play with villainous main characters. See if you can make the villains likable and, if you add in a hero, see if you can make the hero unlikable.

Scene 1: The List

VANESSA: *(Addressing a person offstage.)* Yes, Ms. Byers. Did I mention how pretty you look today? I love that sweater. Love it!

REAGAN: God, you lay it on thick.

VANESSA: My high school career depends on that old witch.

REAGAN: Yeah, but how do you do that without puking?

VANESSA: With difficulty. But **I just have to get the lead in the musical this year. Must. No exceptions. It's mine. And if that means flattering that old bag, that's what I'll do. A few sentences of complete lies will lead to a lifetime of happiness and superstardom.**

REAGAN: How do you figure that? I think that's a bit of a stretch.

VANESSA: **You have no imagination. There are so many ways this could be a springboard for future fame and fortune. Number one: I get agents to come to the play, they sign me up; I become a star. Number two: I get into a great performing arts college, star in their productions; I become a star. Number three: We perform these plays for competitions, I win, and either number one or two happens from there. It's simple. You just need to envision it. I have greater scope than you, Reagan. That's why I'm going to succeed.**

REAGAN: If success means kissing teachers' butts, I'm fine being a loser.

VANESSA: And that's exactly what you will be.

REAGAN: Thanks a lot.

VANESSA: I'm just telling the truth. You are what you tell yourself. As long as you have these lame "morals" about being ethical, you'll always hold yourself back. There will always be people like me who will happily say a few butt-kissing words here and there and get your promotions, raises, and take credit for your work.

REAGAN: But that's why you stink. You don't earn what you get. Everything you get is done through deception and lying. I don't want to be like that. I want to be an honest person. And I think that in the end that will make me a winner. Because people who are smart will recognize that when I give a compliment, it's the truth. They will see that I'm reliable and I actually *do* work rather than just talking about how hard it is all the time. I'm going to be a team player and not a diva. *That's* what's going to set me apart. *That's* how I'm going to succeed.

VANESSA: Please.

REAGAN: You don't think it's possible? I can see you're phony. I can't believe that no one else can. You're going to get a nasty surprise one day, Vanessa, then we'll see who the winner is. One day when you least expect it, your tactics won't work anymore. Maybe it will be some guy you're crazy about thinking you're phony or maybe it will be some movie director thinking you're fake. But one day it will happen.

VANESSA: You're forgetting one thing, Reagan.

REAGAN: What's that?

VANESSA: I'm an excellent actress. I'll never get caught.

REAGAN: But doesn't it bother you that you have to lie all the time? Doesn't it make you sick to your stomach to have to say things you don't mean like telling frumpy Ms. Byers that you *love* her sweater that's coated in cat hair and has a coffee stain on it and was probably crocheted by her half-blind grandmother? God, I swear I would puke if I had to say something like that.

VANESSA: Well, that's the difference between you and me.

REAGAN: I guess so.

VANESSA: So why are you friends with me if I repulse you so much? Does talking to me make you want to puke?

REAGAN: I don't know why we're friends sometimes. I guess you're lucky that you're amusing most of the time.

VANESSA: I feel very fortunate. What would I do without you?

REAGAN: I wonder that myself.

VANESSA: I would probably become completely evil.

REAGAN: Probably.

VANESSA: You need me as much as I need you. Without me you'd be dull, dull, dull.

REAGAN: Maybe so. The list goes up today, doesn't it?

VANESSA: That's right.

REAGAN: So after today you can lay off the "Ms. Byers, you're the most beautiful woman in the world" crap?

VANESSA: Well, it will have to continue a bit since she's directing the show.

REAGAN: I don't know how you do it.

VANESSA: You would if you paid attention. Isn't there anything, Reagan, that's worth doing anything to get? Love? Money? Fame? Recognition? Attention? Anything?

REAGAN: I don't think so. I don't know why you take everything so seriously.

VANESSA: But it's fun. It's a game. Everyone's got their trigger, right? That one thing that loosens them up, makes them think favorably of you. For some people, if you say, "You're so smart," they'll do anything for you. For others, it's telling them how attractive, fashionable, athletic, or charming they are. You just have to know everyone's trigger and the world is yours. It's a fun game. Like Sabrina Mathis.

She would never talk to me, right? So I figured out that she thought she drew really well. One day I was like, "Oh, Sabrina, I saw that drawing you did in chemistry class, it was sooo good," and she was mine forever after that. She'd show me her drawings so she'd get more compliments. People are so needy. So obvious.

REAGAN: So what's my "trigger"?

VANESSA: It's so obvious, Reagan. Don't tell me you don't know.

REAGAN: Intelligence?

VANESSA: Honesty. Integrity. You think you've got better values and ethics than anyone on earth.

REAGAN: Well, I've got you beat by a mile.

VANESSA: Well, duh. It's not exactly what interests me.

(EMMY enters.)

EMMY: (Addressing a person offstage.) Mr. Collins, did you get a haircut? No? Lose weight? God, you just look so great!

(VANESSA crosses toward EMMY.)

VANESSA: (Addressing a person offstage.) Mr. Collins! Hi! It's Vanessa! You look great! Really studly!

REAGAN: Oh my God, I'm totally going to vomit.

VANESSA: What?

REAGAN: Did you say studly? That's gross. He has a *moustache*, Vanessa. He's, like, fifty years old.

VANESSA: Do we have to go through this all over again? He's also musical director for the show. So just get over it already.

EMMY: They're going into a meeting right now to decide on the final casting. I'm going to be the lead.

VANESSA: I don't think so.

EMMY: Why?

VANESSA: Because I'm better than you.

EMMY: We'll see soon enough, won't we?

VANESSA: Have you seen Ms. Byers yet today?

EMMY: She's wearing new glasses.

VANESSA: How did I miss that? Oh, well, it doesn't matter. I complimented her on her sweater.

EMMY: She hates that sweater. Her grandmother made it—

REAGAN: I knew it!

EMMY: —and she hated her grandmother because she never wanted her to be an actress.

REAGAN: So why does she wear the hideous thing?

EMMY: She has poor circulation and the sweater's

warm. Didn't you ever notice that her fingers turn blue sometimes?

VANESSA: Well, yeah, just like I noticed that her hair-cut is circa 1982, but that's not the kind of thing you mention to a person.

EMMY: I suppose that's wise. You're not the kind of person people open up to.

VANESSA: What do you mean by that?

EMMY: People tell me their secrets. I have a very open, honest face. But you . . . not so much.

VANESSA: What does *that* mean?

EMMY: It means exactly what I said.

VANESSA: Listen, you little hobbit, I'm going to get the lead in this play.

EMMY: Not if I have anything to do with it.

REAGAN: Oh my God, you've met your match, Vanessa.

VANESSA: I don't think so. This little worm has no idea what I'm capable of.

REAGAN: Look, Ms. Byers and Mr. Collins are putting the list up!

EMMY: Already? That was a quick meeting.

VANESSA: I guess the choice was obvious.

REAGAN: There's only one way to find out.

Scene 2: The Victor

(VANESSA is tied to a chair with a lot of rope.)

VANESSA: Where am I?

EMMY: Does it matter?

VANESSA: Yes!

EMMY: My basement.

VANESSA: What am I doing here?

EMMY: You're my prisoner.

VANESSA: I don't think so.

EMMY: I do.

VANESSA: Help!

EMMY: Don't bother screaming.

VANESSA: Too late.

EMMY: This is a soundproof recording studio. My parents gave it to me for my birthday.

VANESSA: Why am I here?

EMMY: Ha, ha, ha, ha, ha. As if you don't know.

VANESSA: You want to keep me a prisoner here until the school musical is over.

EMMY: You're not as dumb as you look.

VANESSA: It's hard to look smart in a miniskirt.

EMMY: True.

VANESSA: You have a flaw in your plan.

EMMY: What's that?

VANESSA: What about my friends and family looking for me?

EMMY: I got a geek to hack into your e-mail. You've recently told your parents that you joined a harem. I hope you tan because the desert tends to be a little toasty.

VANESSA: I tend to burn.

EMMY: You took a large bottle of suntan lotion with an SPF of forty-five with you.

VANESSA: Damn!

EMMY: So you see, my plan is brilliant.

VANESSA: It's OK. I'd give it a B minus.

EMMY: How dare you!

VANESSA: You've forgotten one thing.

EMMY: I've forgotten nothing!

VANESSA: Silly little Emmy. Your plan will fail. You see, I would never wear harem pants. They make your thighs look fat. Anyone who knows my fashion sense would see through your little plan.

EMMY: Ah-ha! But I also said that you were going to stop in Paris for slimming beauty treatments not yet available in America!

VANESSA: Damn! Exactly what I would have done. Well, I guess you think you're pretty smart.

EMMY: I *know* I am.

VANESSA: So what exactly do you plan on doing with me for the next months while you rehearse, perform, go to theater competitions . . .

EMMY: As I see it, you're my little plaything. Why don't you sing something for me?

VANESSA: *(Singing.)* I feel pretty! Oh so pretty!

EMMY: Stop! That's enough.

VANESSA: You know I'm better than you.

EMMY: Don't be ridiculous. I stopped you because you're revolting.

VANESSA: *(Singing.)* Don't cry for me Argentina—

EMMY: Silence!

VANESSA: Perhaps you'd like to record this for posterity, since I'm going to be a star.

EMMY: Not if I have anything to do with it!

VANESSA: You can't stop me. Sooner or later you'll have to set me free or I'll escape! You can't keep me here forever. My talent cannot be contained. I cannot be silenced. I am destined for greatness, and no one, not even you, can stop me from meeting my fate. I sparkle. I shine. That's why I got the part and you didn't. I'm afraid I'm just better. I'm sorry to have to say it, but it's true. See? That was good acting. I didn't mean that. I'm not sorry at all! I'm glad that as soon as I get out of this pathetic excuse for a soundproof recording studio I'm going to be a celebrity and make you look pathetic. You'll never win. I'm clever, Emmy, don't you forget that.

EMMY: I wouldn't dream of it. In fact, I expect you to try to escape so I've taken some extra measures.

VANESSA: See? You're scared of me.

EMMY: Don't try that psychology crap with me! I invented it.

VANESSA: No, you didn't. You're not that old. Or are you?

EMMY: I bet I'm younger than you.

VANESSA: If you are, then you've aged very poorly. Nature has not been kind to you.

EMMY: I have the skin of a twelve-year-old!

VANESSA: Yes! Covered with acne!

EMMY: Not true! I have the skin of a . . . an infant!

VANESSA: You're fat!

EMMY: You will rue the day you met me, Miss Vanessa Woodward. This time you will not defeat me. Year after year, I've seen you getting all the things I've wanted—attention, awards, solos—but no more. I've been watching you, and I've learned. I haven't *just* picked up your methods of manipulation and deception—oh no—I've improved and perfected them on a level you've never even dreamed of. No one thinks sweet little Emmy has an underhanded bone in her body. So now, I am going to demolish you. You are going to be blubbering and drooling like a ninety-year-old man who . . . is very sad and drooly when I'm done with you! You will wish you were never born. You will dream of inventing a time machine so you can go back to a time when you didn't know the name Emmy Emmettsonvilleham-Schwartz-Lichtenstein!

VANESSA: I'm already inventing a time machine right now so I can go back to a time when I didn't know the name Emmy Emmettsonvilleham-Schwartz-Lichtenstein, and then when I do know the name Emmy Emmettsonvilleham-Schwartz-Lichtenstein, I will kill said person so that *I* will be the lead in the school play!

EMMY: You don't have that kind of scientific ability.

VANESSA: Oh don't I?

EMMY: No.

VANESSA: And I don't suppose I know anyone who does?

EMMY: No. Unless maybe Harvey Battersea—

VANESSA: Yes! Harvey Battersea will invent it for me!

EMMY: Why would he do that?

VANESSA: Because I will compliment his intelligence and tell him I love his laugh.

EMMY: He snorts when he laughs and has an asthma attack. No one's that good at lying.

VANESSA: I am!

EMMY: Nonsense! Besides, how will you kill me after you go back in time? We met when we were seven. Are you telling me you'd kill a seven-year-old?

VANESSA: I would get you sent to a wilderness program at thirteen, which would break your spirit.

EMMY: You wouldn't dare! My nails!

VANESSA: Oh, I would.

EMMY: You're evil.

VANESSA: I know.

EMMY: I'm beginning to respect you.

VANESSA: We are cut from similar cloths. Except mine

is of better quality. Yours is like a rayon blend and mine is silk.

EMMY: Ridiculous. Your cloth is like sweaty polyester and mine is like breathable cotton. Refreshing and light. Appropriate for every occasion.

VANESSA: Don't you wish.

EMMY: I don't need to wish. Wishing is for losers.

VANESSA: So you must do it a lot.

EMMY: You're so funny I forgot to laugh.

VANESSA: What if Ms. Byers and Mr. Collins don't make you my replacement? Did you ever think of that?

EMMY: They will.

VANESSA: And if they don't?

EMMY: Then you'll have some company.

VANESSA: I know the entire score to *Company*.

EMMY: Not as well as I do!

(VANESSA and EMMY both sing "Another Hundred People," each trying to sing it faster than the other. REAGAN enters.)

REAGAN: What's going on here?

VANESSA: Reagan! I knew I'd be saved!

(REAGAN begins to untie VANESSA.)

EMMY: How did you know?

REAGAN: Vanessa would never wear harem pants! Her thighs would look huge, even after European slimming treatments!

VANESSA: Thanks a lot! They just wouldn't be flattering on anyone. It's not that *my* thighs exclusively would look huge!

REAGAN: Whatever. Do you want me to get you out of here or not?

EMMY: But this studio is soundproof!

REAGAN: I don't know who told you that, but I could hear you two all the way down the block.

EMMY: My parents will die!

REAGAN: Listen, could we hurry this up? I've got rehearsal.

VANESSA: For what?

REAGAN: With both of you missing, Ms. Byers and Mr. Collins had new auditions. I tried out for the heck of it. They said I was the most talented student they'd seen in all their years of teaching. I'm the lead in the school play now.

EMMY: So, how would you look in harem pants?

REAGAN: Well, my thighs are pretty slim.

VANESSA: And you tan very well.

REAGAN: Yes. So?

TALK BACK!

1. What's the difference between admiration and jealousy? Why can you admire someone for the exact same reason you're jealous of another person?

2. Do you think there's a limited or unlimited amount of success and luck to go around? Why?

3. Do you think some people are born lucky or destined to succeed? Why or why not? What, other than talent, makes one person more likely to succeed than another?

4. If you had a time machine, what would you change in your life and why?

5. Why do you think so many people want to work in creative and glamorous fields that receive public attention like fashion, acting, and art? Is it for love or attention or something else?

BAND ON THE RUN

1F, 4M

WHO

FEMALES
Sally

MALES
Bracken
Leon
Marty
Skylar

WHERE Outside.

WHEN Scene 1: Afternoon; Scene 2: Night, the next week.

 Get inside your character's skin. Fill in the character sheet in the back of the book and do some observation from life. Find people who share qualities your character has. Observe how they move and talk. Look for any repetitive gestures or facial expressions. If you can, talk to them and find out how they think. Take some representative qualities and use them to build your character.

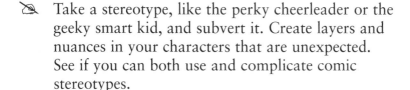 Take a stereotype, like the perky cheerleader or the geeky smart kid, and subvert it. Create layers and nuances in your characters that are unexpected. See if you can both use and complicate comic stereotypes.

Scene 1: Proposition

(Two Goths, BRACKEN and MARTY, sit brooding. SKYLAR enters.)

SKYLAR: So here's the money.

BRACKEN: For what?

SKYLAR: For playing at my party?

BRACKEN: What?

SKYLAR: For playing at my party, idiot. Like we talked about.

BRACKEN: We never talked about that.

SKYLAR: I don't know if you think this is funny, dork, but this is a done deal. You'd better show up.

BRACKEN: I don't know what you're talking about, Skylar!

SKYLAR: OK. I'll try to speak slowly so you can understand. Maybe you're high or something. You'd better not be on the day of the party, that's all I have to say. *(Speaking very slowly.)* The other day, I saw you playing your guitar in front of the guitar store on Grover Street. Against my better judgment and since you didn't suck, I asked you to play some Nirvana-type stuff at my party next weekend. You said sure. I said I'd pay you two hundred dollars. You said give me a hundred up front and I said no way. So I agreed to fifty up front, and I would kill you if you didn't show up and do an amazing set. So here's your freakin' money, freak. You'd better do an amazing job. I live at twenty-five Sycamore. Next Saturday. Nine o'clock.

BRACKEN: I'm not in a band. I don't play guitar.

SKYLAR: Jesus, what was I thinking hiring a bunch of Goth freaks? This is the kind of crap I was afraid of.

BRACKEN: I don't know what you're talking about.

SKYLAR: How much more can I tell you? I mean, were you out of it then or now? You're playing at my party next weekend. And don't try to pretend you're not. I saw and heard you playing your guitar. I know you have a band because that's what you dorks do since you don't have a social life. You sit around writing songs about how your insides hurt and no one understands you and that kind of crap. So show up and don't suck or I'll kill you. It's that simple.

(MARTY takes the money from SKYLAR.)

MARTY: No problem, Skylar.

SKYLAR: Thank you. Weirdos. Good day, gentlemen. I suggest you start practicing so you're alive in two weeks' time.

MARTY: You bet.

(SKYLAR exits.)

BRACKEN: What are you doing?

MARTY: Getting fifty dollars! What do you think I'm doing?

BRACKEN: Skylar Ridge thinks we're going to play at his party next weekend. He thinks we're in a band. He thinks we play instruments.

MARTY: He thinks *you* play guitar. He didn't say anything about me.

BRACKEN: Great. Great!

MARTY: What?

BRACKEN: What? We don't do any of those things. So he's going to kill us.

MARTY: He won't *kill* you.

BRACKEN: Us.

MARTY: You.

BRACKEN: Yes, he will!

MARTY: No. Kill? He'd go to prison. He'll just beat you up or something.

BRACKEN: Oh, that's so much better.

MARTY: He won't even do that.

BRACKEN: You don't think he'll follow through? I don't think he'll have any moral qualms about beating us to a pulp.

MARTY: You. To a pulp. But he won't. He obviously has you confused with someone else.

BRACKEN: Well, no kidding.

MARTY: So when he goes to kill someone, he'll find some other Goth kid.

BRACKEN: He must think we all look the same. We don't all look the same! How could he possibly think that? That's the whole point. We all look different. We're nonconformists, rebels, anarchists. So, by definition, we're all different, right? We don't wear the same old junk that all the other kids in school wear. We're not trying to be just like the popular crowd. We despise those people. They're sad. We're making our own rules. Doing things our own way. No one's like us. We're individuals. There's nothing similar about us.

MARTY: Except we all wear black and makeup and dye our hair and get piercings and tattoos—

BRACKEN: But *different* tattoos and *different* piercings.

MARTY: There are only so many places to get pierced.

BRACKEN: My shoulder blades are pierced.

MARTY: So are mine.

BRACKEN: Yeah, but *he* doesn't know that. And I doubt the guy he thinks is me has his shoulder blades pierced.

MARTY: Does your mom ever grab you by the hoops on your back? Mine does.

BRACKEN: Ah-ha! Mine are studs.

MARTY: So we are different.

BRACKEN: Yeah. We're not all buying our clothes at the mall and that kind of conventional crap.

MARTY: You bought that shirt at the mall.

BRACKEN: Yeah, OK, this shirt is from the mall, but I didn't buy it at Abercrombie and Fitch or anything. I got this shirt at a skater store, which is totally unexpected since I'm not a skater, then I individualized it. See this tear? I did that. It didn't come like that. So no one has a shirt like this one. I'm completely unique, see?

MARTY: Cool. Hey, I've got this new idea. I'm going to be so conventional that I'll be unconventional.

BRACKEN: What?

MARTY: I'm going to start speaking in clichés and junk so I'm unconventionally conventional.

BRACKEN: That makes no sense.

MARTY: Does it make no sense or does it make so much sense it's blowing your mind?

BRACKEN: It makes no sense.

MARTY: The early bird gets the worm. You'll be wishing you thought of it next year.

BRACKEN: Clichés are stupid.

MARTY: Clichés are clichés because they're true.

BRACKEN: Shut up.

MARTY: I'll be as silent as the grave. Silence is golden. It's always darkest before the dawn.

BRACKEN: That doesn't even apply.

MARTY: Doesn't it?

BRACKEN: We're getting off the subject. What am I going to do about this band thing? It's not like I can learn guitar in a week.

MARTY: Like I said, it's always darkest before the dawn.

BRACKEN: Stop that!

MARTY: When one door closes, another opens. Or a window. Or something. Desperation is the mother of invention.

BRACKEN: You made that one up.

MARTY: No, I didn't. Or maybe I did. I am a mystery even to myself.

BRACKEN: Listen, can you just be normal for one second? I'm in trouble here and I could use a little help.

MARTY: Speak to me, my son.

BRACKEN: You're turning into a priest.

MARTY: I was thinking more Mother Superior from *The Sound of Music*. My mom used to make me watch that every Easter when I was little. It was sick.

BRACKEN: No wonder we get beat up. Even I think that's gay.

MARTY: Not that there's anything wrong with that.

BRACKEN: Except it doesn't get us any girlfriends.

MARTY: Being in a band would.

BRACKEN: Yeah, but we're not in a band, stupid.

MARTY: You're starting to sound like Skylar.

BRACKEN: I'm just trying to be sensible.

MARTY: I'm just saying, what if we did play at his party? We could collect the rest of the money.

BRACKEN: What if the other guy shows up? And we've taken his fifty-dollar advance payment?

MARTY: He won't show up.

BRACKEN: How can you be sure?

MARTY: Skylar had to tell us where he lived. So, presumably, he didn't tell the other guy.

BRACKEN: OK, but that still doesn't solve that we can't play instruments and we don't have a band.

MARTY: Oh, ye of little faith. Genius is one percent inspiration and ninety-nine percent perspiration.

BRACKEN: Are you suggesting we don't cut P.E. class today?

MARTY: I'm suggesting we put together some kind of makeshift band.

BRACKEN: But won't we suck?

MARTY: We'll turn up the sound really high. It'll all be reverb. No one will know.

BRACKEN: I don't know about this.

MARTY: You don't trust me?

BRACKEN: You're not very reliable.

MARTY: People in glass houses shouldn't throw stones. And people wearing eyeliner should be in a band. This is going to work out just fine. I don't know why we never thought of it sooner!

Scene 2: Par-tay

(BRACKEN and MARTY enter with guitar cases.)

BRACKEN: I don't think this is a very good idea, Marty. We really have no idea what we're doing.

MARTY: We just need to yell and jump around a lot. We'll be fine.

BRACKEN: I really think maybe you're selling musicians short. I think there's a little more to it.

MARTY: No, there's not. Do you want that hundred and fifty dollars or not?

BRACKEN: We never should have taken that fifty-dollar advance. We knew we weren't the people he hired to do this gig. That's what they call it, don't they? A gig? I don't even know the lingo! Lingo sounds really stupid, too. Jargon? Syntax? Colloquialism? I'm not cut out to be a rock star! I don't know what I'm saying! I'm not cool, Marty. I'm just not. I mean, I want to be, just like the next guy—OK, I admit it—but I'm cut out for brooding and sitting in corners, not for standing in front of a lot of people and making an ass out of myself.

MARTY: Please. You make an ass out of yourself daily, Bracken.

BRACKEN: Thanks for the encouragement. I feel a lot better now. Let's just do it, then.

MARTY: OK.

BRACKEN: I was *joking*. Joking! Ever heard of jokes?

MARTY: I've heard of jokes; I just haven't heard one yet. Do me a favor and never become a comedian.

BRACKEN: **I don't think your taking in the enormity of this situation! Not only could Skylar beat the crap out of us if he figures out we suck, the *entire* party of people, popular jock-type people, could collectively beat the crap out of us. This is no good. We need to run.**

(LEON enters. He's a type-type, too.)

LEON: Hey, guys, does some uptight jock named Skylar live here?

MARTY: Yeah.

LEON: You know, he asked me to do a gig here, then he never gives me any cash in advance or his address. Genius. Too many tackles on the football field. But it looks like he's got the cash to spare. Maybe I'll hit him up for more, eh? *(Beat.)* What are you guys doing here? You weren't invited, were you?

BRACKEN: No, no. We were leaving. We, uh, live nearby.

LEON: Yeah, I didn't think so. No way would the guy I met be hanging with guys like us. He probably thinks we'd give him cooties.

MARTY: So, do you have a band or something?

LEON: Yeah. I gotta call them with the address.

(SKYLAR enters.)

SKYLAR: What are you dorks doing out here? Shouldn't you be setting up inside? I want the music to start *soon,* and it better not suck or you're dead.

LEON: You never gave me an address or the advance money. You're lucky I showed up.

SKYLAR: What are you talking about? I gave you fifty bucks. And you're here, so I gave you the address, dumbass. What kind of game are you trying to play here?

LEON: Are you trying to cheat me? Because you just cost yourself a band.

SKYLAR: I gave you the money and now I expect you to play!

LEON: I don't think so.

SKYLAR: Are you sure you want to start this, skinny, because I will finish it.

LEON: Are you threatening me? You cheat me out of my advance money, I take the trouble to try to find out where you live, and this is the thanks I get? I'm not calling my band. We're not playing. It was going to be cool, I thought we had a deal, but I will not be disrespected. That's all there is to it. And if you lay a finger on me, I'm calling the police.

SKYLAR: My dad gives generously to the Police Athletic

League. I think they'll be very sympathetic toward me, freak.

LEON: My dad's a police officer, tough guy. So just try me. You jock types think you rule the world. I've got news for you, buddy. You're no better than me. I just dare you to lay a finger on me. I've got connections. I can have the cops here busting your party up for underage drinking so fast that your head would spin on your big, fat neck.

SKYLAR: Your dad is not a police officer.

LEON: Wanna bet? Try me. I'm not scared of you.

SKYLAR: Why don't you just get your band inside and play, buddy. I don't want any trouble.

LEON: Right.

SKYLAR: I paid you, so just finish the job, and you'll get the rest.

LEON: My guys aren't coming.

SKYLAR: Dude, your guys are standing right next to you.

LEON: These are not my guys.

SKYLAR: Are you trying to mess with my mind? They've got guitars in their hands.

LEON: I don't know these dudes, *dude.* My band is waiting to hear from me on the locale.

SKYLAR: So call them.

(SKYLAR looks at BRACKEN. Then he looks at LEON. Then he looks at BRACKEN again.)

SKYLAR: Who? Whose? *(Beat.)* I gave *you* the money, dude.

BRACKEN: What? I don't know what you're talking about.

LEON: Are you trying to steal my gig?

BRACKEN: What? No. I don't even play. This is his brother's roommates' guitar. I'm just . . . carrying it.

SKYLAR: You're just carrying a guitar.

BRACKEN: Right.

SKYLAR: That's weird.

BRACKEN: Well, I'm a freak, remember?

LEON: So what did you do with my fifty bucks?

BRACKEN: What? Nothing. It wasn't me, I mean! Nothing.

MARTY: He got a tattoo.

BRACKEN: What? What are you saying?

MARTY: Look, as I see it, you have two choices. You can get beat up by the jock or this other guy. I'd pick him. *(Indicates LEON.)*

BRACKEN: You are a great friend. You take the money in the first place and convince me this is a good idea, and now this.

LEON: Know what? I don't even want a fight. I'm not that kind of person. If you want the gig, you go for it. I have other things I could do.

BRACKEN: No, no, no! It was yours. It's OK. I'll find a way to pay you back the fifty. It's all yours. We'll go now.

LEON: No, no. I'm outta here. I've been out so much this week my mother's starting to think I'm happy 'cause I have some friends. So I'd better get home and dispose her of that idea before she starts making cookies and asking when my "little friends" are coming over. Later.

(LEON exits.)

BRACKEN: No! No! Wait! No!

SKYLAR: Shut up. Just get inside and play.

BRACKEN: No. Wait. I can't.

SKYLAR: Why?

BRACKEN: I broke my finger before I got here.

SKYLAR: That's too bad. One time I played an entire football game on a sprained ankle. So get inside and set up now before I kill you.

BRACKEN: My father's, uh, head of the mafia in this town. I wouldn't kill me if I were you.

SKYLAR: Shut up, loser. Everybody knows *my* dad is the head of the mafia in this town.

(SKYLAR exits.)

BRACKEN: Let's run.

MARTY: Where? We go to the same school as him. We have to see him sometimes.

BRACKEN: We don't even have a drummer!

MARTY: I told you, my cousin is coming.

(SALLY enters. She is very clean-cut.)

MARTY: There she is. Right on time.

BRACKEN: She? That is your cousin?

SALLY: Hey.

BRACKEN: You're joking, right?

MARTY: No.

SALLY: Is something wrong?

BRACKEN: We're going to go in there with the two of us and her.

MARTY: Right.

SALLY: What's the problem?

BRACKEN: You're a girl and you look like *that*.

SALLY: You have a problem with how I look?

BRACKEN: We're supposed to be a *band*.

MARTY: Dude, she's the only one of us who's had more than two music lessons in her life.

SALLY: Try seven years.

MARTY: She's doing us a favor.

BRACKEN: Yeah, but look at her.

SALLY: Remember, you promised me sixty bucks out of this.

BRACKEN: Sixty? No way. We divide it evenly. In fact, we should get more.

SALLY: You guys? Why? I am saving your butts. I could be doing something better than going through this disaster.

BRACKEN: If we get beat up, *we* get beat up. Not you.

SALLY: Whose fault is that? You accepted this gig. Frankly, I can't believe you showed up.

MARTY: I need money.

SALLY: Your mom told you to stop buying those ceramic dolls already. You're too old.

MARTY: They're figurines. And they're collectable. They'll be worth millions one day.

SALLY: Right.

BRACKEN: That's what this is about? Figurines? Oh my God, I am going to be killed by the mafia so you can buy figurines.

MARTY: They'll be worth something someday. You'll wish you had them.

(SKYLAR enters.)

SKYLAR: Get moving, dorks! I want music now!

(SKYLAR exits.)

BRACKEN: I hate you, Marty. I really do.

SALLY: Come on, guys, hurry up. Let's get my drum set in there and get this over with. The piercings on my shoulder blades are itching.

MARTY: What? *I* have piercings on my shoulder blades.

SALLY: So? It's not like you invented it.

BRACKEN: No way! I thought that was the one thing that made me original. Now every normal kid must be doing it. I started it, though.

SALLY: As if. My sister's best friend's roommate's brother had it done, like, ten years ago.

BRACKEN: That's not possible. No way.

SALLY: Well, it is possible. And by the way, what makes you think that "every normal kid" is getting their shoulder blades pierced?

BRACKEN: Well, you did.

SALLY: What makes you think I'm normal? You shouldn't judge people on how they look. I happen to be *so* normal, *so* average that I'm completely unconventional.

MARTY: Hey, that's my thing! You stole my thing!

SALLY: You snooze, you lose, cousin. The early bird catches the worm.

MARTY: Hey—

SALLY: Shut up, Marty. Let's just do this.

TALK BACK!

1. What would you do if you were Bracken? Would you take the money? Would you show up at Skylar's party?

2. Do people have any expectations about you based on how you look or dress? Are these assumptions true or false?

3. Do you think people act in accordance to their looks or that people's looks are influenced by their personality? For example, if a person looks tough, do they have a tough personality or have they adapted their personality to fit with their looks?

4. Are people's personalities influenced by their name? For instance, can you be a sensitive artist named Butch?

5. Was there ever a point where you consciously decided to go against any assumptions your parents made about you and/or your role in your family? Why?

6. Why do people get tattoos and piercings? What do you think it says about a person's personality when they get a tattoo or piercing?

GYPSIES

3F, 5M

WHO

FEMALES
- Alberta
- Magenta
- Johanna

MALES
- Giuseppe
- Gianni
- Matt
- Pete
- Roberto

WHERE Scene 1: Pete's bedroom; Scene 2: The woods.

WHEN Night.

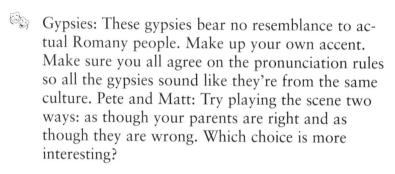 Gypsies: These gypsies bear no resemblance to actual Romany people. Make up your own accent. Make sure you all agree on the pronunciation rules so all the gypsies sound like they're from the same culture. Pete and Matt: Try playing the scene two ways: as though your parents are right and as though they are wrong. Which choice is more interesting?

Take another childhood myth (this one is "be good or the gypsies will steal you away") and use it as the basis of a play, for example, "if you cross your eyes, they'll stay that way."

Scene 1: Kidnapped!

(MAGENTA climbs in through the window. PETE is sleeping in bed.)

MAGENTA: Hello.

(PETE wakes up, sees MAGENTA.)

PETE: Hello?

(PETE rubs his eyes.)

PETE: Hellooo.

(PETE pinches himself to make sure MAGENTA is real.)

PETE: Ouch! Well, hello there!

MAGENTA: *(Impatiently.)* Yes, hello, hello. We are here to kidnap you.

PETE: What?

MAGENTA: I see now. You cannot hear. *(Louder.)* We are here to kidnap you!

PETE: I heard you. I just don't know why.

MAGENTA: There needs to be a why?

PETE: Well, yeah. I kinda think you have the wrong address or something. There's just me and my parents here, and they're not rich or anything.

MAGENTA: You are Pete.

PETE: Yes.

MAGENTA: Then no mistake. We kidnap you.

PETE: I'm not a kid.

MAGENTA: You are not a man, either. Close enough.

PETE: I'm closer to being a man than a kid.

MAGENTA: Yeah, right, kid.

PETE: I happen to be very manly.

MAGENTA: Mm-hmm.

PETE: Really!

MAGENTA: Right. *(Yells out the window.)* Hey! Do I have to do all the work here?

(JOHANNA enters through window.)

JOHANNA: You don't have to yell. What is the problem?

MAGENTA: He ask questions.

JOHANNA: He is Pete?

MAGENTA: He is Pete.

JOHANNA: Pete, we kidnap you.

PETE: As I was explaining to the nice lady here, I am, in fact, a man.

JOHANNA: Absolutely. You big, strong man. Now get moving, Pete. We kidnap you.

PETE: But—

(ALBERTA *climbs through the window.*)

ALBERTA: We go! Come on! I do not have all day!

MAGENTA: He will not go.

JOHANNA: Pete give us problems.

PETE: Ladies, ladies! I have an idea. How about we stay here? All four of us? I can order a few pizzas, we can have something to drink, maybe watch a movie and settle down for a nice, cozy evening right here in my bedroom.

(Beat.)

ALBERTA: No.

PETE: Come on, ladies. Give me a chance! I think we could have a really nice time. Why don't you tell me what you'd like to do? I'm up for anything.

ALBERTA: How about kidnapping?

PETE: No, no kidnapping. Seriously. You cannot kidnap me. I'm not a kid! I'm a man. I've been through puberty. I've got testosterone pumping through my body. Did I show you my guns? *(He flexes his biceps and kisses them.)*

ALBERTA: Yes, yes. We are very impressed.

PETE: OK, great. So we're agreed. We just chill here and have a really nice time, just me and you ladies. I'm thinking we can all slip into something more comfortable and we can get some backrubs going. I am totally at your service.

ALBERTA: OK! Enough—how you say?—chitchat.

PETE: I couldn't agree with you more. Enough talk. Time for some action!

(ALBERTA, MAGENTA, and JOHANNA grab PETE and start pulling him toward the window.)

PETE: Oh my God, I've dreamed about this! I'm in heaven!

JOHANNA: Oh shut up.

PETE: Just be gentle, ladies! There's plenty of Pete to go around!

MAGNETA: Out the window with you.

PETE: What?

(GIUSEPPE enters.)

GIUSEPPE: What's the holdup?

PETE: Whoa. I didn't sign up for this. I thought we had an understanding, ladies! What's going on?

ALBERTA: Giuseppe, the stupid boy, he will not go out the window.

JOHANNA: He refuse to be kidnapped!

MAGENTA: He think he is a man.

(Beat. GIUSEPPE looks PETE over carefully then bursts out laughing.)

JOHANNA: Giuseppe, stop. Is not funny. I am very tired. Do we kidnap this Pete or no? Magenta, Alberta, and I are just sexy gypsy girls. We need a big strong man like you to take the stupid boy out the window.

PETE: How many times do I have to tell you—I'm not a boy! Or a kid! I'm too old to be kidnapped by gypsies!

JOHANNA: You see how he talk, talk, talk. I am getting one of my headaches, Giuseppe.

GIUSEPPE: No! Not the headaches!

JOHANNA: Yes, the headaches! You know I cannot do the sexy gypsy dancing with the veils and the juggling swords when I have the headaches. So pick the silly boy up and help us, Giuseppe. It is the least you can do. I scrub the floor. I cook the meals. I wear the gypsy skirt that hide my beautiful legs so you no get jealous. All I ask is you take out garbage and carry stupid boy. Is this too much for big, strong man like you?

GIUSEPPE: Why you nag me, woman?

JOHANNA: No, never mind. I see it is too much. Maybe you not so big and strong a gypsy. Maybe your brother Gianni is the bigger, stronger gypsy. Maybe *he* let me wear miniskirt.

PETE: I'll let you wear a miniskirt!

GIUSEPPE: Shut up, stupid boy! Fine, woman. I take boy. But you do dance with veils tonight!

JOHANNA: Maybe. But no sword juggling.

GIUSEPPE: We go now.

(GIUSEPPE firmly grasps PETE.)

PETE: Help! Mom! Dad!

Scene 2: Prisoner!

PETE: What do you plan on doing with me!

GIUSEPPE: Dunno.

PETE: You're not . . . going to eat me?

ALBERTA: No, stupid boy.

PETE: *(Laughing, relieved.)* Oh. I just heard once—

ALBERTA: You too stringy.

> *(ALBERTA, GIUSEPPE, MAGENTA, and JO-HANNA laugh.)*

MAGENTA: Good one, Alberta.

GIUSEPPE: We should do something before the others arrive.

PETE: Others?

JOHANNA: You think we are the only gypsies?

PETE: Well, no, but . . .

MAGENTA: I have idea! We have boy dance while we wait.

PETE: But this nice lady here *(Indicates JOHANNA.)* I hear she does a mean veil and sword-juggling act.

GIUSEPPE: You want to see Johanna's veil and sword dance?

PETE: I think that would be very nice, yes.

GIUSEPPE: That is dance she does only for me! You think, little Pete, she will do dance for you?

PETE: No, no! I didn't know! I just thought . . . I heard you say . . .

GIUSEPPE: I kill any man who will see Johanna's veil and sword dance!

PETE: Well, now that I think about it, I'm not very interested—

GIUSEPPE: What? She no good enough for you? Johanna, do dance for boy!

PETE: No! No! No dance for boy! I mean, you're very beau—nice, but I think we should, um, play charades!

MAGENTA: I think boy should dance for Magenta.

ALBERTA: And Alberta! Dance, boy.

PETE: But—

GIUSEPPE: Dance!

(PETE busts a move, breaking out some old dance moves like a robot. He's pretty terrible and embarrassing to watch. After a minute, he's run out of dance moves. He slows down and stops. All stare at him in silence.)

ALBERTA: You stink.

PETE: There's no music! I'm not prepared. I've never had any dance lessons!

ALBERTA: Man, something stinks in here. Smells like . . . Pete.

(ALBERTA, GIUSEPPE, MAGENTA, and JOHANNA laugh.)

PETE: I didn't have any warning. Seriously, you guys, why did you kidnap me? My parents are going to be looking for me, you know. So don't get any big ideas.

MAGENTA: *(In a high-pitched voice.)* "Oh, no! Where is my little Pete? I am Pete's mommy and I miss his stinky dancing!"

ALBERTA: "Something is wrong! There is oxygen in the house! Oh, Pete is not here sucking it all up with his talk, talk, talk!"

(ALBERTA, GIUSEPPE, MAGENTA, and JOHANNA laugh.)

PETE: Hey!

JOHANNA: We have the news for you, Pete. Your mommy and daddy pay for us to take you.

PETE: What?

GIUSEPPE: We start—how you say?—brat camp.

PETE: What? Why?

MAGENTA: We gypsies fall on hard times. All that make us special you take away. We wear the gypsy skirts. Everybody wear the gypsy skirts! We wear the hoop earrings. Everybody wear the hoop earrings! We wear the bandana. Everybody wear the bandana! We do not even know who is gypsy anymore. So we got to find new way to be special.

GIUSEPPE: And to make the money.

MAGENTA: So we think—what do we gypsies know better than anyone else? And we think—the woods! Our ancestors live in this woods for years. We know every inch! Ask me anything. Ask me which direction for nearest Wal-Mart.

PETE: Which direction for nearest Wal-Mart?

MAGENTA: *(Pointing to her left.)* That direction. Twelve miles after you pass the tree with bones of babies we eat.

(ALBERTA, GIUSEPPE, MAGENTA, and JOHANNA laugh. PETE joins in.)

PETE: Yeah, how did that rumor ever get started anyway?

GIUSEPPE: I guess 'cause we eat babies.

(PETE laughs weakly. No one laughs with him. Beat. ALBERTA, GIUSEPPE, MAGENTA, and JOHANNA laugh.)

ALBERTA: They taste so good!

(ALBERTA, GIUSEPPE, MAGENTA, and JO-HANNA laugh.)

MAGENTA: Anyway, back to my story. So we start wilderness brat camp in woods to make us money and so we add to the society. Welcome to our little camp, Pete! We going to make you nice boy.

PETE: I am a nice boy! Why would my parents send me here? I don't believe you!

MAGENTA: You on drugs. The crack, the crank, the weed, the X, the LSD, the—

PETE: No, I'm not!

ALBERTA: Yes, you are. Look at you, pathetic druggie.

PETE: No! You've got me mixed up with someone else.

JOHANNA: How many time we have to go through this? You are Pete, yes?

PETE: Yes!

JOHANNA: You are boy we kidnap and take off drugs.

PETE: But I'm not on drugs.

JOHANNA: Your mother think you on drugs.

PETE: I'm not.

JOHANNA: Whatever.

PETE: What do you mean, whatever? I want to go home!

MAGENTA: *(In a high voice.)* "Oh, look, I'm Pete! I miss my mommy!"

ALBERTA: *(In a high voice.)* "I want to go hooome!"

PETE: I don't talk like that!

MAGENTA: *(In a high voice.)* "I don't talk like that!"

PETE: Stop it!

ALBERTA: *(In a high voice.)* "Stop it!"

(GIANNI and MATT enter. GIANNI is a super-suave gypsy.)

GIANNI: Here is other stupid boy.

MATT: I'm not a stupid boy! I'm a man.

GIANNI: Right, right.

JOHANNA: See, Giuseppe? Gianni get boy all by himself. He does not need three sexy gypsy girls to help him.

GIUSEPPE: Gianni, Gianni, Gianni! You love Gianni so much, go gypsy dance for him!

GIANNI: If I see one more veil and sword dance, I will puke.

MATT: Will someone please explain what's going on here?

PETE: Well, these are gypsies, and—

ALBERTA: Faster!

PETE: *(Speaking very quickly.)* —they started a wilderness-type camp for kids who—

GIANNI: Less words!

PETE: You on drugs!

MATT: No, I'm not!

PETE: They think we are!

MATT: Well, I'm not!

PETE: Neither am I!

GIUSEPPE: So. You not on drugs? This is not what your parents tell us. They say you sit in room day and night. All alone in the dark, with the shades down. You come out with glassy, bloodshot eyes just to eat. You difficult. You ungrateful. You argue. This we know for fact! You sloppy and filthy and listen to stupid music that sound like noise. You never want to go to the school. You do not like to wash. Your toenails grow long. Did I mention the stupid, stupid music? But your parents, they read pamphlet. They look at checklist. Antisocial—check! Red eyes—check! Bad attitude—check! Grades falling—check! They your parents. They know you. They see you on drugs.

Look at you! What you do in your room all day and night? Drugs!

MATT: No! I'm playing video games and I'm on the Internet!

PETE: We got a Victoria's Secret catalogue last week!

GIUSEPPE: Lies! This is not just teenager stuff! You boys be *very* annoying! You need discipline! You need toughening up! You need fresh air and muscles! You need attitude adjustment! So you in brat camp now, boys. We straighten you out!

MATT: We're teenagers! What do you expect?

ALBERTA: Your parents expect good, sweet boys who clean room and talk nice. Not two big-mouth slobs like you.

PETE: Hey, you can't talk to me like that! I've had enough of this!

GIANNI: The boy is right. You can't talk to him like that!

PETE: That's right!

GIANNI: So I tell you to shut your big mouth, smelly slob.

PETE: Hey!

ALBERTA: Gianni, you lucky you a beautiful gypsy man. You too macho.

GIANNI: Impossible!

MAGENTA: He has a point.

ALBERTA: Magenta!

MAGENTA: Well, he is very sexy gypsy man.

(ROBERTO enters.)

ROBERTO: I'm baaack!

GIANNI: Roberto!

ROBERTO: So, these are our boys?

GIUSEPPE: Yes.

ROBERTO: They are very stringy.

JOHANNA: Yes.

MATT: We're not on drugs.

PETE: We insist on going home!

ROBERTO: You insist? You insist?

(Tense beat. ALBERTA, GIUSEPPE, MAGENTA, JOHANNA, and ROBERTO laugh.)

ROBERTO: Ooo. He a funny boy. Dance for me, boy!

ALBERTA: Oh no, no, no! He terrible.

ROBERTO: What about other boy?

JOHANNA: We do not know yet.

ROBERTO: OK. *(Indicates PETE.)* He juggle swords. *(Indicates MATT.)* He do dance with veils.

PETE: I can't juggle swords!

MATT: Isn't dancing with veils a girl thing?

ROBERTO: It amuse me.

MATT: Don't we have a choice here?

ROBERTO: What—you think you can find way out of the woods?

MATT: Well—

PETE: There's a Wal-Mart to the left of the tree with the baby bones.

MATT: The what?!

ROBERTO: You going to walk twelve miles?

PETE: Well, maybe. I could if I wanted to.

ROBERTO: I think you better start juggling, boy.

GIANNI: Tell you what. I like you. I give you hint. Don't stand right under swords when you juggle. That way you only lose maybe a finger or a toe.

MATT: This is a nightmare!

ROBERTO: Dance, pretty boy!

TALK BACK!

1. Many old wives' tales and fairy tales were designed to control children. Are there any myths your parents told you when you were a kid to get you to behave?

2. If you wanted to prevent someone else from doing one of your bad habits, what would you say? For example, I bite my nails. I might tell someone the nails can rip up the lining of your stomach and kill you.

3. Have your parents ever falsely accused you of any wrongdoings? What was it and why do you think they suspected you? Were you able to clear your name?

4. What is the biggest misconception about teenagers?

5. What do you think about so-called brat camps where juvenile delinquents get sent into the wilderness to learn survival techniques and to correct their behavior? Do you think they can work? Do you think this is a good method to reform wayward teens?

6. What scared you when you were a kid? Do those fears still linger or are you over them?

APPENDIX

CHARACTER QUESTIONNAIRE
FOR ACTORS

Fill in the following questionnaire as if you are your character. Make up anything you don't know.

PART 1: The Facts

NAME:

AGE/BIRTHDATE:

HEIGHT:

WEIGHT:

HAIR COLOR:

EYE COLOR:

CITY/STATE/COUNTRY YOU LIVE IN:

GRADE*:

BROTHERS/SISTERS:

PARENTS:

UPBRINGING (strict, indifferent, permissive, etc.):

* If you are an adult, what educational level did you reach (college, medical school, high school, etc.)?

PART 2: Rate Yourself

On a scale of 1 to 10 (circle one: 10 = great, 1 = bad), rate your:

APPEARANCE	1 2 3 4 5 6 7 8 9 10
IQ	1 2 3 4 5 6 7 8 9 10
SENSE OF HUMOR	1 2 3 4 5 6 7 8 9 10
ATHLETICISM	1 2 3 4 5 6 7 8 9 10
ENTHUSIASM	1 2 3 4 5 6 7 8 9 10
CONFIDENCE	1 2 3 4 5 6 7 8 9 10
DETERMINATION	1 2 3 4 5 6 7 8 9 10
FRIENDLINESS	1 2 3 4 5 6 7 8 9 10
ARTISTICNESS	1 2 3 4 5 6 7 8 9 10

Do you like yourself?	YES	NO
Do you like your family?	YES	NO
Do you like the opposite sex?	YES	NO
Do you like most people you meet?	YES	NO

Which of the following are important to you and which are not? Circle one.

WEALTH	Important	Not Important
KNOWLEDGE	Important	Not Important
POWER	Important	Not Important
PEACE	Important	Not Important
POPULARITY	Important	Not Important
LIKABILITY	Important	Not Important
LOVE	Important	Not Important
SPIRITUALITY/RELIGION	Important	Not Important

PART 3: Favorites

List your favorites (be specific).

FOOD:

SONG:

BOOK:

MOVIE:

TV SHOW:

CITY:

SEASON:

COLOR:

PIECE OF CLOTHING:

SMELL:

ANIMAL:

SOUND:

SCHOOL SUBJECT:

PLACE:

PERSON (historical or living):

PART 4: Describe Yourself

Circle all words/phrases that apply to you:

SHY	OUTGOING
OUTDOOR TYPE	INDOOR TYPE
POSITIVE	NEGATIVE
PARTY PERSON	COUCH POTATO
HOMEBODY	LEADER
FOLLOWER	MOODY
CALM	SILLY
HAPPY	SAD
RELAXED	ENERGETIC
INTELLECTUAL	CLEVER
NEAT	MESSY
FUNNY	HONEST
SNEAKY	DISHONEST
OPEN-MINDED	JUDGMENTAL
CARING	CREATIVE
PRACTICAL	WILD
CAREFUL	WELL-LIKED
ARTISTIC	LAZY
OPINIONATED	IMAGINATIVE
REALISTIC	DRAMATIC
STREETWISE	TOLERANT
HARD-WORKING	SPONTANEOUS
STRONG	BRAVE
CURIOUS	QUIET
CHATTY	DARK
SUNNY	DISAPPOINTING
HOPEFUL	UNDERSTANDING
KIND	BORED
DIFFICULT	COMPLICATED
SWEET	POWERFUL
MACHO	ENTHUSIASTIC
GIRLY	INSECURE
LUCKY	PICKY
DISADVANTAGED	FRIENDLY
GOSSIPY	ANGRY
SECRETIVE	WISHY-WASHY
INDEPENDENT	GEEKY
WEAK	COOL
NURTURING	ANNOYING
REBELLIOUS	GOOD

PART 5: Truth/Dreams

If I die tomorrow, people will remember me as a:

One thing that really annoys me is:

My worst habit is:

I'm really scared of:

My parents think I'm:

When I grow up, I want to be*:

Superpower I'd most like to have:

The thing I'd most like to change about myself is:

My greatest talent is:

I'd most like to travel to:

Three professions I'd like to try:

The title for the story of my life would be:

* If your character is an adult, what is your character's job and does he or she enjoy it?

PLAYWRIGHT'S CHECKLIST

Does my play have:

☐ Conflict?

If everyone gets along, not much happens! It's important to have conflict in any play, comedy, or drama.

☐ Character development?

Do the characters change at all in the course of the play for better or worse? It's interesting to the audience to see some variety in character. We all act differently in different situations, so it makes sense for a character to become more complex when he or she is faced with conflicts.

☐ Plot twists?

What could be more exciting than being surprised by a plot twist you hadn't expected?

☐ Believable dialogue?

Even if the characters are strange and out-of-this-world, make sure the dialogue sounds something like the way people actually speak to one another. Any character voices you create must remain consistent throughout. For example, if a character is very intellectual and proper, having them say "I ain't gonna go" is going to seem very out of place.

☐ A strong sense of place and time?

Especially when you don't have a big set and costumes, it's important to make the play's setting clear.

☐ Characters you can relate to?

Every play has at least one character the audience can understand and sympathize with. A good way to create conflict is to put this "normal" character in the path of another character that is odd, otherworldly, or downright horrible!

SCENE ELEMENTS WORKSHEET

Answer these questions for each scene you do.

WHO: (Who are you?)

WHERE: (Where are you?)

WHEN: (Is this the past, present, or future? Day or night?)

WHY: (Why are you where you are?)

OBJECTIVE: (What do you want?)

ACTIONS: (What do you do to get what you want? For example, beg, flatter, pressure, and so on.)

CHARACTER TRAITS: (What are you like as a person?)

RELATIONSHIP: (What are your relationships to the other characters?)

OBSTACLES: (What or who stands in the way of your objective?)

EXPLORATION GAMES

Draw a picture of your character(s).

Improvise a scene before the play begins or after it ends.

Dress as your character(s) to see how it changes your behavior.

Make the scene or play into a musical or an opera.

Listen closely to everyone around you during a scene.

Try to make your acting partners respond to your behavior.

Lead with a different body part: in other words, change which part of your body enters the room first and pulls you forward when you walk. Leading with your nose can make you seem pompous, leading with the top of your head can make you seem insecure, etc.

Change the speed/rhythm at which you speak or move.

Decide who you like and who you don't like in the scene; don't be afraid to show it.

Change your volume (whisper or speak out loudly).

Make your voice higher or lower in pitch.

Notice who's taller and who's shorter than you in the scene; let this affect you.

Change your accent.

Sit down with another actor to make up your characters' past lives together.

Do an activity you think your character might do.

Do a chore around the house the way your character might do it.

Write a diary entry, a letter of complaint, or a personal ad as your character.

Come up with a gesture that your character does habitually.

THE AUTHOR

Kristen Dabrowski is an actress, writer, acting teacher, and director. She received her MFA from The Oxford School of Drama in Oxford, England. The actor's life has taken her all over the United States and England. Her other books, published by Smith and Kraus, include *111 Monologues for Middle School Actors Volume 1*, *The Ultimate Audition Book for Teens 3*, *20 Ten-Minute Plays for Teens*, and the *Teens Speak* series. Currently, she lives in the world's smallest apartment in New York City. You can contact the author at monologuemadness@yahoo.com.